THE VICTORY ACCORDING TO MARK

THE VICTORY ACCORDING TO MARK

AN EXPOSITION OF THE SECOND GOSPEL

BY MARK HORNE

 Canon Press ■ Moscow

Mark Horne, *The Victory According to Mark:*
An Exposition of the Second Gospel
© 2003 by Mark Horne
Published by Canon Press, P.O. Box 8741, Moscow, ID 83843
800-488-2034 / www.canonpress.org

03 04 05 06 07 08 09   9 8 7 6 5 4 3 2 1

Cover design by Paige Atwood

Printed in the United States of America.

Library of Congress Cataloging–in–Publication Data

Horne, Mark.
The Victory According to Mark / Mark Horne
p. cm.
Includes bibliographical references and index.
ISBN 1-59128-007-9 (pbk.)
1. Bible. N.T. Mark—Commentaries. I. Title.
BS2585.52 .H67 2002
226.3'07—dc21   2002015017

While my debts to many for the content of this book are mentioned in the epilogue, I would like to dedicate this book first to my wife Jennifer and to my children, who all sacrificed a great deal of time for me to get this done and offered encouragement. Without them there would be no book.

I would also like to include in this dedication Jim and Janey Irwin and all the saints who met in our weekly Bible study at their house in Renton, WA. where I first began to develop this material.

MARK HORNE

Contents

Mark 1:1-15

The Call

> He comes to us as One unknown, with-
> out a name, as of old, by the lakeside, He
> came to those men who knew Him not.
> He speaks to us the same word: 'Follow
> thou Me!' and sets us to the tasks which
> He has to fulfill for our time. He com-
> mands. And to those who obey Him,
> whether they be wise or simple, He will
> reveal Himself in the toils, the conflicts,
> the sufferings which they shall pass
> through in His fellowship, and as an in-
> effable mystery, they shall learn in their
> own experience Who He is.
>
> —Albert Schweitzer

Mark's beginning is characteristically succinct. "The beginning of the gospel of Jesus Christ, the Son of God."
The danger here is that we are so accustomed to
speaking of and reading about a "gospel," or even "the
gospel," and also "the Son of God," that we don't bother to think
about what these terms meant in their original context.

WHAT IS THE GOSPEL? (1:1)

Let's take the term "gospel" first: What does it *mean*? We kick the
word around a lot in evangelical circles. It is derived from the Old English word *godspell* and is used to translate the Greek term, *evangelion*.
The best transliteration of the term is "good news" or "joyful message."
However, we might have a better understanding if we consider some
prominent ways in which the word was used at the time of Jesus.

THE PAGAN CONTEXT

Consider this inscription from 9 B.C.:

> The providence which has ordered the whole of our life, showing concern and zeal, has ordained the most perfect consummation for human life by giving to it Augustus, by filling him with virtue for doing the work of a benefactor among men, and by sending in him, as it were, a deliverer for us and those who come after us, to make war to cease, to create order everywhere ...; the birthday of the god [Augustus] was the beginning for the world of the *glad tidings* that have come to men through him.[1]

Here we have the announcement of the birthday of Augustus Caesar dubbed as a gospel—"glad tidings" or *good news*. As Biblical and historical scholar N. T. Wright sums up the evidence, "In the Greek world, as is well known among scholars, *evangelion* is a regular technical term, referring to the announcement of a great victory, or to the birth, or accession, of an emperor."[2]

The point here is that a "gospel" refers to a *public announcement of victory*.

THE JEWISH BACKGROUND

Wright also points out two passages from Isaiah which bear on the original meaning of the word "gospel." The first is Isaiah 40:9 (I include verse ten for context).

> Get yourself up on a high mountain,
> O Zion, bearer of *good news*.
> Lift up your voice mightily,
> O Jerusalem, bearer of *good news*;
> Lift it up, do not fear.
> Say to the cities of Judah,
> "Here is your God!"
> Behold, the Lord God will come with might,
> With His arm *ruling* for Him.

---

[1] N. T. Wright, *What Saint Paul Really Said* (Grand Rapids: Eerdmans, 1997), 43. A slightly different reading of the same inscription is found in John Dominic Crossan's *Jesus: A Revolutionary Biography* (New York: HarperCollins, 1994), 1.

[2] Ibid.

Behold, His reward is with Him,
And His recompense before Him. (emphasis added)

In the common Greek translation of the Hebrew scriptures, the word for "good news" is *evangelion*. The same is true of Isaiah 52:7.

How lovely on the mountains
Are the feet of him who brings *good news*,
Who announces peace
And brings *good news* of happiness,
Who announces deliverance,
And says to Zion, "Your God *is King!*" (emphasis added)

These texts are about a return from exile for God's people when their land will be returned to them and God will again dwell in their midst on Zion in Jerusalem in the Temple. It is important to remember that the Temple was God's palace. In fact, the same Hebrew word is used throughout the narrative of 1 Kings and 1 Chronicles to describe the construction of both God's "Temple" and King Solomon's "palace." Both structures are given the same name because they are both royal houses wherein a king is enthroned. At the time of the exile, God abandoned his palace and allowed Nebuchadnezzar to destroy it. Instead of ruling from there, He came on his throne and dwelt with the exiles in Babylon, as revealed in Ezekiel 1.

Thus, prophesying the return from exile when God's presence will again be in Jerusalem is an announcement of his enthronement. It fits in quite well with the pagan use of the term in the first century. Both Jew and Gentile alike use the term to refer to the victory or ascension of a king—perhaps the triumphant beginning of his rule. For the Jews this meant the one true God who had chosen a people and chosen to dwell enthroned among them at the Temple in Jerusalem. For the pagans it meant some *other* god had begun to rule as king—often these false gods were mighty men like Caesar who claimed to be divine.

THE CHRISTIAN PROCLAMATION

What is the upshot of all this? Quite simply, while the gospel *does* result in changed lives and forgiven individuals, the gospel message is *not* simply a method for changing one's life or receiving forgiveness. In other words, the gospel is not a description of how one goes about getting "a personal relationship" with God. When a new king has conquered and, as a result, ascends to his throne to rule, the news causes his enemies to tremble in fear. It causes those who want to benefit from his rule to bow their knees in submission to his authority. That is the kind of news the gospel is. That is what Mark is writing about—the conquest and triumph of a new king.

THE MEANING OF CHRIST

In our culture today I suspect many people probably think that "Christ" was simply Jesus' last name. That is quite wrong, of course. Christ comes from the Greek word for "anointed." It is the equivalent of the Hebrew term for "Messiah"—God's promised king.

Again, this is a *royal* title. While other officials in Israel's society were anointed with oil in order to call them into office, the anointing of kings gained special prominence. Samuel anointed Saul with oil to set him apart for the kingship of Israel (1 Sam. 10:1). David was then anointed by Samuel when God decided to take the kingdom from Saul and give it to him. It is important to note that this anointing was not precisely the same thing as a coronation ceremony, since neither Saul nor David was able to assume the throne immediately after he was anointed. Nevertheless, it was considered the starting point in the calling of the king and the basis of his rule. Thus, Psalm 89:20 stresses, "I have found David My servant; with My holy oil I have anointed him." And in Psalm 2 :2, David or a Davidic king is referred to as the Lord's "anointed." When Samuel tells Saul, "the Lord anointed you king over Israel," he is saying that God has *made him king* of Israel. Anointing is the essential element in giving Saul his identity as one called to be king.

Thus, if you want to explain what the term "Jesus Christ" means, perhaps a good paraphrase would be "King Jesus." That would certainly be a good way to begin such an explanation. The word "Christ" is a term for his royal status as a descendant of David.

SON OF GOD

The term "son of God" fits well within this royal language. God had promised David,

> When your days are complete and you lie down with your fathers, I will raise up your descendant after you, who will come forth from you, and I will establish his kingdom. He shall build a house for My name, and I will establish the throne of his kingdom forever. I will be a father to him and he will be a son to Me; when he commits iniquity, I will correct him with the rod of men and the strokes of the sons of men, but My lovingkindness shall not depart from him, as I took it away from Saul, whom I removed from before you. And your house and your kingdom shall endure before Me forever; your throne shall be established forever. (2 Sam. 7:12–16)

From that time on, and perhaps even before, being God's "son" was a royal title. All Israel was called God's son (Exod. 4:22; Hos. 11:1). It was appropriate that the king, as the representative of his people, should also bear that same title for himself. Thus, while Psalm 2 ultimately points to Jesus and His resurrection (Acts 13:33), it also describes David and his dynasty to the initial readers and hearers: "Surely I will tell of the decree of the LORD: You are my son; today I have begotten you." Likewise, we read in Psalm 89:20–27,

> I have found David My servant;
> With My holy oil I have anointed him,
> With whom My hand will be established;
> My arm also will strengthen him.
> The enemy will not deceive him,
> Nor the son of wickedness afflict him.
> But I shall crush his adversaries before him,
> And strike those who hate him.
> And My faithfulness and My lovingkindness will be with him,
> And in My name his horn will be exalted.
> I shall also set his hand on the sea,
> And his right hand on the rivers.
> He will cry to Me, "*You are my Father,*
> My God, and the rock of my salvation."
> I also shall make him *first-born,*
> The highest of the kings of the earth. (emphasis added)

To be the Son of God is to be Israel's king. Thus, in John's Gospel we see the two titles put side by side: "Nathanael answered Him, 'Rabbi, You are the Son of God; You are the King of Israel'" (Jn. 1:49). Mark's Gospel gives us the same idea. There are some manuscripts which are missing the reference to "son of God," but whatever the original reading of Mark, the idea is still quite present: *This is the story of the victory of Jesus, the king of Israel.*

THE BEGINNING

Since we have analyzed every other word in Mark's short introduction, perhaps we should consider if there is anything to be said about the first one: "the beginning." Given the overtones of royalty that we have already dealt with, it may be profitable if there is a royal Davidic connection with Mark's use of this term.

Jeff Meyers, in his 1997 lectures on Mark's Gospel, suggests that there is such a connection. Bearing in mind that Mark is about to quote a prophecy of making "ready the way of the Lord" and "making his paths straight," we may have here a suggestion of Solomonic wisdom: "The fear of the Lord is the beginning of knowledge" (Prov. 1:7a).

What follows in Proverbs is a sustained exhortation to avoid evil company. "My son, do not walk in the way with them. Keep your feet from their path" (1:15). Rather, the "son" should

walk in the way of good men,
And keep to the paths of the righteous.

For the upright will live in the land,
And the blameless will remain in it;
But the wicked will be cut off from the land,
And the treacherous will be uprooted from it. (2:20–22)

Later Solomon sums up the need for a choice of the right way:

The *beginning* of wisdom is: Acquire wisdom;
And with all your acquiring, get understanding.
Prize her, and she will exalt you;
She will honor you if you embrace her.
She will place on your head a garland of grace;
She will present you with a crown of beauty.

Hear, my *son*, and accept my sayings,
And the years of your life will be many.
I have directed you in the *way* of wisdom;
I have led you in upright *paths*.
When you walk, your steps will not be impeded;
And if you run, you will not stumble.
Take hold of instruction; do not let go.
Guard her, for she is your life.
Do not enter the *path* of the wicked,
And do not proceed in the *way* of evil men. (4:7–14; emphasis
added)

As we follow the way of the Lord through Mark, we will find
the basic choice of which way to go to be presented rather strik-
ingly, especially in irony and parable and in other ways which remind us of royal wisdom.

THE PROPHECIES (1:2,3)

When Paul preached to the Pisidian Antiochians, he summed up
his message by announcing the gospel and then quoting prophecies
of the gospel.

> And we preach to you the good news [gospel] of the promise made
> to the fathers, that God has fulfilled this promise to our children
> in that He raised up Jesus, as it is also written in the second Psalm,
> "You are My Son; today I have begotten you." (Acts 13:32, 33)

Likewise, the beginning of Paul's letter to the Romans follows
that same form, first mentioning the gospel and then the prophecies: "Paul, a bond-servant of Christ Jesus, called as an apostle, set
apart for the gospel of God, which He promised beforehand
through His prophets in the holy Scriptures." The author of Hebrews, also, first announces the identity of Jesus as God's Son and
promised one (vv. 1–4) and then begins quoting Scriptural prophecies (vv. 5ff.).

By announcing a gospel and then backing it up with Hebrew
prophecies, Mark seems to be following the Apostolic presentation
quite closely.

> The beginning of the joyful proclamation of Jesus Christ, the Son
> of God.

As it is written in Isaiah the prophet:

"Behold, I send My proclaimer before Your face,
Who will prepare Your way;
The voice of one crying in the wilderness,
'Make ready the way of the Lord,
Make His paths straight.'"[3]

This may seem like a rather straightforward prophecy, but it is actually not. What Mark has done is quote a verse from Isaiah with an introductory verse from Malachi. The angel or messenger sent to prepare the way comes from Malachi 3:1. The voice in the wilderness is found in Isaiah 40:3.

But things are even more complicated. Mark does not quote Malachi 3:1 verbatim, but subtly alters it. Consider them together:

Malachi 3:1—Behold, I am going to send My angel, and he will clear the way before My face.

Mark 1:2—Behold, I send My angel before Your face, who will prepare Your way.

Now some of the differences could simply be the result of translating from Hebrew to Greek. However, the Malachi prophecy has God saying that His angel will prepare the way for himself. Mark has God sending an angel to prepare the way for someone else. Why is Mark changing the passage?

I would suggest[4] that Mark is intentionally combining a passage from Exodus with the passage from Malachi in order to introduce the prophecy from Isaiah.

Exodus 23:20—Behold, I am going to send an angel before you to guard you along the way, and to bring you into the place which I have prepared.

---

[3] I diverged from the NASB by translating "angel" or "messenger" (the same word) as "proclaimer." I also translated "gospel" as "joyful proclamation." I am trying to show the close relationship between verses 1 and 2 anchored in the similarity between *evangelion* ("good news" or "gospel") and *angellon* ("angel" or "messenger").

[4] Following Austin Farrar, *A Study in Saint Mark* (New York, Oxford Univ. Press, 1952), 55.

Malachi 3:1—Behold, I am going to send My angel, and he will clear the way before My face.

Mark 1:2—Behold, I send My angel before Your face, who will prepare Your way.

What do these two Old Testament passages mean, taken together as an interpretation of Isaiah's prophecy? The passage from Exodus is God's promise to Moses to lead the Israelites by His angel through the wilderness away from Egypt to the Promised Land. The prophecy of Malachi is God's promise to once again visit His people in a visible way for salvation and judgment.

God did not give a prophecy to Malachi that only happened to accidentally sound like his words to Moses. God's Word is not prone to accidents. There are similarities between what the people desired at the time of Malachi and what they were hoping for in the wilderness. The people of Israel in the wilderness were not simply moving to a better place; they were moving to a place where God promised to dwell with them.

> Behold, I am going to send an angel before you to guard you along the way, and to bring you into the place which I have prepared. Be on your guard before him and obey his voice; do not be rebellious toward him, for he will not pardon your transgression, since My name is in him. But if you will truly obey his voice and do all that I say, then I will be an enemy to your enemies and an adversary to your adversaries. For My angel will go before you and bring you into the land of the Amorites, the Hittites, the Perizzites, the Canaanites, the Hivites and the Jebusites; and I will completely destroy them. (Exod. 23:20–23)

Notice that God's presence, mediated by His angel bearing His name, is the key to their victory and acquisition of a new land. That angel was the Lord Himself who had led them out of Egypt as a pillar of cloud by day, and a pillar of fire by night (Exod. 13:21), the same angel who, in a flaring cloud, protected the Israelites from the Egyptian army (Exod. 14:19), and the same angel who descended on that dark cloud upon Mount Sinai (Exod. 19:16). Indeed, Moses sums up their entire journey through the wilderness by saying, "when we cried out to the Lord, He heard our voice and sent an angel and brought us out from Egypt" (Num. 20:16). That angel, of course, is the Lord Jesus himself, the one whom Mark's Gospel is written about.

It is important to remember that the Angel of the Lord dwelt within the Tabernacle Moses built. God's presence with His people was the whole point of the structure. As he told Moses, "Let them construct a sanctuary for Me, that I may dwell among them" (Exod. 25:8). After the Tabernacle was built, the cloud on Mount Sinai moved into it (Exod. 40:34–38). When God threatened to only lead them out of the wilderness at a distance, Moses was not happy.

> Then the Lord spoke to Moses . . . "Go up to a land flowing with milk and honey; for I will not go up in your midst, because you are an obstinate people, lest I destroy you on the way." . . . Then Moses said to the Lord, "See, You say to me, 'Bring up this people!' But You Yourself have not let me know whom You will send with me. Moreover, You have said, 'I have known you by name, and you have also found favor in My sight.' Now therefore, I pray You, if I have found favor in Your sight, let me know Your ways, that I may know You, so that I may find favor in Your sight. Consider too, that this nation is Your people." And He said, "My presence shall go with you, and I will give you rest." Then he said to Him, "If Your presence does not go with us, do not lead us up from here. For how then can it be known that I have found favor in Your sight, I and Your people? Is it not by Your going with us, so that we, I and Your people, may be distinguished from all the other people who are upon the face of the earth?" (Exod. 33:1a, 3, 12–16)

The reason Moses was not happy was that acquisition of the Land, as important as that was, was not of much value to him if God was not with them. Essential to the program of entering the Promised Land was doing so with God's visible presence in their midst. Without God's presence in the Tabernacle in the middle of the twelve tribes of Israel, the trip was simply not worth making.

This helps us understand why God gave Malachi a prophecy which reminded the hearers and readers of Exodus 23:20. In Malachi's day the Israelites were back in the Land after the return from exile. They had rebuilt the Temple—even though it was relatively dinky (Ezra 3:12, 13). There priests were serving God in His house.

And yet something was wrong. The Land was in jeopardy due to Israel's new sins (Mal. 4:6b). The Temple was not being treated as it should have been treated (Mal. 3:10). The priests were corrupt (Mal. 2:1–9). Despite dwelling in a special land, where God's servants served Him in His dwelling palace, *there was a real sense in which God was absent rather than present.* Geographically, the situation for Malachi was completely unlike the situation for Moses. He was in the Promised Land whereas Moses was in the wilderness. Yet covenantally, the nation of Israel was just as much in the wilderness as the generation of Moses had been. They needed God's presence. Only when He visibly visited His Temple would they truly possess the blessings that God had promised them. As long as God was outside of the Land, in a sense, then so were they, no matter where they were geographically located.

When God promised Moses He would send an angel before them, He was promising to be present with them and lead them out of the wilderness into a place of communion with Himself. In a sense, Malachi is prophesying the same thing. God will end the time of wilderness wandering by entering the Land, coming to His Temple, saving those who trust in Him, and destroying those who do not. For Malachi, as is the case for the Gospel writers, Jerusalem and the Land now count as Egypt and the wilderness. God must re-enter the land for it to truly be the Promised Land. Even though Malachi's people are already settled geographically, they still need to be saved by God's presence and put in the real Land. God's coming to His Temple is, in a real sense, their exodus out of Egypt and entry into the land. By coming into the Land Himself, God is bringing His people into the Promised Land.

All of this is necessary if Mark's readers are going to understand his invocation of Isaiah 40:3.

> The voice of one crying in the wilderness, "Make ready the way of the Lord, Make His paths straight."

Mark has already alluded to this passage by speaking of his document as a "gospel." By quoting this passage Mark is not simply extracting an *ad hoc* prooftext but offering a comprehensive explanation for who Jesus is and why John the Baptist preceded Him.

He is also giving his readers a hint of what is going to happen in
the rest of his story. The only way to grasp this is to have this portion of Scripture firmly in mind. Let us read it together:

> "Comfort, O comfort My people," says your God.
> "Speak kindly to Jerusalem;
> And call out to her, that her warfare has ended,
> That her iniquity has been removed,
> That she has received of the Lord's hand
> Double for all her sins."
>
> A voice is calling, "Clear the way for the Lord in the wilderness;
> Make smooth in the desert a highway for our God.
> Let every valley be lifted up,
> And every mountain and hill be made low;
> And let the rough ground become a plain,
> And the rugged terrain a broad valley;
> Then the glory of the Lord will be revealed,
> And all flesh will see it together;
> For the mouth of the Lord has spoken."
> A voice says, "Call out."
> Then he answered, "What shall I call out?"
> All flesh is grass, and all its loveliness is like the flower of the field.
> The grass withers, the flower fades,
> When the breath of the Lord blows upon it;
> Surely the people are grass.
> The grass withers, the flower fades,
> But the word of our God stands forever.
>
> Get yourself up on a high mountain,
> O Zion, bearer of *the gospel*.
> Lift up your voice mightily,
> O Jerusalem, bearer of *the gospel*;
> Lift it up, do not fear.
> Say to the cities of Judah,
> "Here is your God!" (emphasis added)

The odds are that, if you are a Christian reader, you have been
taught—correctly—that this is a prophecy of Jesus Christ and His
ministry. But we need to do some study to understand *how it works*
as a prophecy. Isaiah's original readers would have—again correctly—read this passage in the context of Isaiah's own life and its
place in his book. The last thing mentioned just before this prophecy is Isaiah's confrontation with Hezekiah:

Then Isaiah said to Hezekiah, "Hear the word of the Lord of hosts, 'Behold, the days are coming when all that is in your house, and all that your fathers have laid up in store to this day shall be carried to Babylon; nothing shall be left,' says the Lord. 'And some of your sons who shall issue from you, whom you shall beget, shall be taken away; and they shall become officials in the palace of the king of Babylon.'" Then Hezekiah said to Isaiah, "The word of the Lord which you have spoken is good." For he thought, "For there will be peace and truth in my days."

It is in the shadow of this prediction of the Babylonian exile that we are given a glorious prophecy that there will be "a highway for our God." This is a promise of a *return from exile* to the Promised Land. Not only is this made clear by the immediate context of Isaiah 39, but from the wider context as well. Early on in Isaiah, the Lord laments that "My people go into exile for their lack of knowledge" (Is. 5:13). Later, Isaiah will explicitly promise the return for the exiles (49:21; 51:14).

Thus the "highway for our God" is *the highway by which He promises to lead the captives away from Babylon back to the Promised Land*. In fact, God through Isaiah explicitly compares the journey from Babylon to the exodus from Egypt.

> Awake, awake,
> Clothe yourself in your strength, O Zion;
> Clothe yourself in your beautiful garments,
> O Jerusalem, the holy city.
> For the uncircumcised and the unclean
> Will no more come into you.
> Shake yourself from the dust, rise up,
> O captive Jerusalem;
> Loose yourself from the chains around your neck,
> O captive daughter of Zion.

> For thus says the Lord, "You were sold for nothing and you will be redeemed without money." For thus says the Lord God, "My people went down at the first into Egypt to reside there, then the Assyrian oppressed them without cause. Now therefore, what do I have here," declares the Lord, "seeing that My people have been taken away without cause?" *Again* the Lord declares, "Those who rule over them howl, and My name is continually blasphemed all day long. Therefore My people shall know My name; therefore in that day I am the one who is speaking, 'Here I am.'"

How lovely on the mountains
Are the feet of him who brings the gospel,
Who announces peace
And brings the gospel of happiness,
Who announces deliverance,
And says to Zion, "Your God is King!" (52:1–7)

The exile among the nations is comparable to slavery in Egypt. God's deliverance, then, will be a new exodus. As Isaiah also writes:

Go forth from Babylon! Flee from the Chaldeans!
Declare with the sound of joyful shouting, proclaim this,
Send it out to the end of the earth;
Say, "The Lord has redeemed His servant Jacob."
And they did not thirst when He led them through the deserts.
He made the water flow out of the rock for them;
He split the rock, and the water gushed forth. (48:20, 21)

The end of exile and return to Israel is explicitly compared to God's delivery of the Hebrews from Egypt and His care for them in the wilderness. The return from exile is a new exodus.

It is that prophecy of a return from exile which Mark is saying ultimately points to the calling and work of Jesus. He begins his writing by saying that his victory announcement is what was written by Isaiah the prophet when Isaiah prophesied the restoration of Israel after their deportation from Babylon.

But what could a return from exile have to do with Jesus' campaign in Palestine? After all, the Hebrews were living in the Promised Land at the time of Jesus. They had a Temple where they could hold their sacred feasts. They had a priesthood. What could a prophecy about the return from exile have to do with Jesus and the Israelites of His day?

In combining Exodus 23:20 with Malachi 3:1 to introduce the quote from Isaiah, Mark has explained the import of the return from exile. Yes, the Israelites are in the Promised Land, just as they were in Malachi's day. Nevertheless, they are covenantally in the wilderness and in exile—somehow back in Egypt and Babylon. In a very real sense they need to be brought back to the Promised Land. Mark has not yet told us why Israel is in such a bad situation, and he probably expects that his initial readers already have some idea. We will have to figure it out as we go along. Nevertheless, it is clear that Israel is in grave danger and needs to be rescued by God. They need God to come to them so that He is once again present with them. Only then will they truly possess God's promise.

WHAT DOES ALL THIS MEAN?

In the first place, we have a hint here of great humility on God's part. Instead of God's people needing to be taken out of the Land and then come back to it out of the wilderness, God Himself seems to be the one undergoing the exile and exodus and returning to the Promised Land. It is not the people who must undergo a literal geographical exile. God is in some sense taking it upon Himself. And Jesus will quite literally take all the weight of oppression by foreign powers upon Himself.

In the second place, we see here a great advancement of the human race. In Exodus 23:20 it is the angel of the Lord—God Himself—who prepares the way for his people to inherit the promises. Yet in Malachi 3:1 the angel is no longer God, but a man as a messenger (again: remember that "angel" and "messenger" are the same word in both the Hebrew and Greek Scriptures). As we will see, like the Angel of the Lord in the wilderness, John the Baptist remains at Israel's eastern frontier in the desert, preparing the people to inherit the land.

More than that, we also see here as clear a statement as we could hope for that Jesus is God Himself. Malachi 3:1 is unambiguous: the messenger will prepare the way for the arrival of Yahweh, "the Lord" as He is usually called in our English Bibles. Yet Mark, like the other three Gospel writers, claims that the messenger is John the Baptist. And Mark is quite clear that it is Jesus for whom John has prepared the way. Jesus is the presence of God coming to His people.

But who can endure the day of his coming? (Mal. 3:2)

Indeed, the prophesy from Isaiah which Mark quotes goes on to promise that every valley will be raised and every mountain will be made low. Mark is warning us of what we will read. We can safely guess that the mountains are not going to be too thrilled about being flattened, even if the valleys do rejoice in being raised.

THE NEW MOSES AND THE NEW JOSHUA (1:4–5)

Having recited the prophecy of the messenger or angel of the Lord who will prepare the way for Jesus, Mark now presents the messenger.

The Jordan was the boundary that marked the transition of the Israelites from the wilderness to the Promised Land. Indeed, when the Israelites miraculously crossed the Jordan on dry ground, they also circumcised all their males since they had not practiced circumcision for the forty years in the wilderness (Josh. 3–5). This was not the only transition point in Israel's exodus that involved passage through a body of water. Earlier, the crossing of the brook Zered marked the point at which the older generation of Israelite warriors died in the wilderness so that the new generation could make a second attempt at entering the Promised Land (Deut. 2:13–15). The text specifically says that the men died because "the hand of the Lord was against them." The first such crossing, of course, did not involve the death of unfaithful Israelites, but rather of the Egyptian army. The crossing of the Red Sea marked the leaving of Egypt forever, just as crossing the Jordan marked the leaving of the wilderness.

BAPTISM

What is the reason for John's baptizing in the Jordan River? The Greek word "baptism" was used to refer to ceremonial cleansings and washings. Mark himself, for example, uses the word to refer to washing dishes (7:4) just as the author of Hebrews uses it to refer to the ceremonial sprinklings of the Mosaic law (Heb. 9:10). However, if only cleansing was involved in John's baptism, then John's geographic location makes no sense. If all that mattered to John's "baptism of repentance for the forgiveness of sins" was the application of water, then there would have been no reason for him to stay in the wilderness in the region of the Jordan. He would have reached many more people by simply going to Jerusalem and preaching there. But for some reason, he felt compelled to baptize in the Jordan and make people go out to him in order to be baptized.

We need to ask ourselves "Why the Jordan?"

The Apostle Paul later refers to the crossing of the Red Sea as a "baptism" (1 Cor. 10:1, 2). Perhaps thinking about why Paul associated crossing a body of water on dry ground with baptism will help us understand why John began baptizing at the Jordan River. If we do that, there is no reason to only consider the Red Sea as if it were the only analogy Paul could have used. If the miraculous crossing at the Red Sea was a baptism, why not also the miraculous crossing at the Jordan River? After all, the Israelites were actually circumcised when they crossed the Jordan River, which Paul elsewhere associates with baptism (Col. 2:11–13). And then we have the water crossing between those two points, the brook Zered, which marked the transition between the condemned generation and the new generation promised the land.

The common factor in these three instances is that the water marks a boundary between the old and the new, the cursed-for-sin and the blessed-with-forgiveness. It is interesting that this corresponds to the layout of the Tabernacle and Temple: one could not enter God's presence without first going by a laver of cleansing (Exod. 30:17ff) or a "bronze ocean" (1 Kgs. 7:23ff). The Israelites passed through the Red Sea and then met with God on Mount Sinai. Once the Tabernacle was built, God's presence dwelt in it, which the priests could only approach through the laver of cleansing. It isn't too hard to see here a common theme: *passing through water means moving closer to where God is and typically involves repentance and abandonment of or deliverance from the old in order to attain the new*. In all likelihood, the primal foundation for the significance of passing through water comes from the "waters above" which God placed under His throne in the heavens (Gen. 1:6–8; cf., Rev. 4:6). Passing through the waters represents going to God's throne from the earth.

As the place where God would dwell enthroned among His people, the Promised Land resembled the heavens where God ruled among the angels. Thus Joshua and the Israelites entered the land by miraculously passing through water and leaving the flesh of the old creation behind in circumcision, just as before Moses and the Israelites had passed through water on their way to God's presence at Sinai, leaving the Egyptians and the plagues of Egypt behind (Exod. 15:26). Following this tradition, those many Judeans, who left their homes and traveled the long road to John the Baptist in order to be baptized at the Jordan River, were *re-entering the Promised Land*. They were confessing for themselves and their children that, even though they were geographically located in Israel, covenantally they were still in the wilderness. Something had gone horribly wrong and they once again needed God's presence to come and lead them out of exile to a place of rest. Like Isaiah surprised by the presence of the Lord in His Temple, who confessed both that he was a man of unclean lips and a part of a people of unclean lips (Is. 6:5), those coming to John for baptism were confessing both that theirs was a sinful, adulterous, and unbelieving generation (Mk. 8:38; 9:19), and that they personally had participated in its sin, adultery, and unbelief. They were admitting that they were still under bondage in Egypt, though Moses had led them out of it so many centuries ago.

FORGIVENESS

It is very important to realize that, though individual concerns were real in John's ministry, his public proclamation of "the forgiveness of sins" had immense public consequences. It is quite easy for a person today to assume that his sins are his personal property which are no one's business but his own and God's. However, the Bible also acknowledges *corporate* sin both in the sense of institutionalized evil and in the sense of the punishment of society rather than only individual wrongdoers. Mark himself has reminded us of this by using Isaiah 40:3 as a prophecy of the ministry of John the Baptist. For in the context of that quote, Isaiah promises blessings for Jerusalem as a city, saying

> "Comfort, O comfort My people," says your God.
> "Speak kindly to Jerusalem;
> And call out to her, that her warfare has ended,
> That her iniquity has been removed."

When we read that John was baptizing for "the forgiveness of sins," we will be misunderstanding the text if we don't immediately think of *national liberation* as well as personal pardon. The

Israelites journeying to the Jordan would have heard that idea in John's proclamation, as would John himself. Mark makes the connection clear by using prophecies of Israel's salvation from Egypt and exile to explain John's vocation. Israel was under God's judgment and John was telling them how it could be removed. Israel needed to be renewed and to repent.

Of course, everyone knew that not everyone would repent. What was hoped was that God would come to Israel and renew her by removing the wicked from her. Mark's citation of Malachi 3:1 underscores this because Malachi goes on to say:

> "Then I will draw near to you for judgment; and I will be a swift witness against the sorcerers and against the adulterers and against those who swear falsely, and against those who oppress the wage earner in his wages, the widow and the orphan, and those who turn aside the alien, and do not fear Me," says the Lord of hosts.

By making the pilgrimage to the Jordan, those who believed John's message showed that they wanted to be visibly separated from those under judgment when the Lord came. They wanted to be members of the future purified Israel. Undergoing John's baptism helped them anticipate that they were not only God's covenant people, but that they would remain in that covenant after God cast others out. In order to be assured that they would be included in the future forgiven Israel whose iniquity would be removed, they needed to repent and ask for personal forgiveness now.

What Mark implies by invoking Isaiah 40 in the context of John's ministry, Luke later made explicit by recording some of John's interaction with those who came to him.

> He therefore began saying to the multitudes who were going out to be baptized by him, "You brood of vipers, who warned you to flee from the wrath to come? Therefore bring forth fruits in keeping with repentance, and do not begin to say to yourselves, 'We have Abraham for our father,' for I say to you that God is able from these stones to raise up children to Abraham. And also the axe is already laid at the root of the trees; every tree therefore that does not bear good fruit is cut down and thrown into the fire." And the multitudes were questioning him, saying, "Then what shall we do?" And he would answer and say to them, "Let the man who has two tunics share with him who has none; and let him who has food do

likewise." And some tax-gatherers also came to be baptized, and they said to him, "Teacher, what shall we do?" And he said to them, "Collect no more than what you have been ordered to." And some soldiers were questioning him, saying, "And what about us, what shall we do?" And he said to them, "Do not take money from any-one by force, or accuse *anyone* falsely, and be content with your wages." (Lk. 3:7–14)

Notice here that John is quoted as warning of "the wrath to come." Mark's use of Malachi 3 gives us the same understanding of John's ministry. When God comes to His Temple, who can with-stand the day of His coming? Notice also that the issue is whether or not one is a member of *the true Israel*. It is not enough to be a descendant of Abraham because every tree that does not bear good fruit will be cut down. Thus, different groups of people ask John what they must do to be identifiable as the true Israel, the true children of Abraham.

By the way, just because John proclaims repentance, doesn't mean he was excluding faith or preaching "legalism." The issue is not whether one can be good enough to earn salvation. Rather, the issue for John and his hearers (and for us in our own situation) is whether or not we can rightfully identify ourselves as the people whom God will mercifully vindicate when He comes to judge the world. If we may behave in a way that God allows us to anticipate that we, to quote the Westminster Shorter Catechism, "shall be openly acknowledged and acquitted in the day of judgement" (question 38), then our activity is not an attempt to earn anything from God or to save ourselves by our own efforts. Rather it is a demonstration that we trust God and thus can hope in Him. As Paul told the Galatians, "we through the Spirit, by faith, are wait-ing for the hope of righteousness." Such a hope has nothing to do with our own merit; the only thing our merits can bring is fear. But that doesn't mean that such a hope may be held by all apart from any conditions. We are required to believe or trust God as He has re-vealed Himself. Thus, the author of Hebrews writes about Moses:

By faith Moses, when he had grown up, refused to be called the son of Pharaoh's daughter; choosing rather to endure ill-treatment with the people of God, than to enjoy the passing pleasures of sin;

considering the reproach of Christ greater riches than the trea-
sures of Egypt; for he was looking to the reward. (Heb. 11:24–26)

This is the kind of faith being demonstrated by those who respond to John's proclamation. They *believe* what he says is true, that
God is about to visit His people. They then *act* on their belief,
knowing that God is going to both judge and save. May we do the
same because we too trust God and believe His message.

JOHN'S VOCATION (1:5–8)

When King Ahaziah heard a description of a man his messengers
had met, he exclaimed, "It is Elijah the Tishbite." That description
of Elijah reminds us now of John the Baptist: "He was a hairy man
with a leather girdle bound about his loins" (1 Kgs. 1:8). It is not
until chapter 9 that Mark reveals explicitly that John corresponds
to Elijah in the prophecy of Malachi 4, but here Mark's description
of John's camel hair clothing with a leather belt around his waist
reminds us of the prophet.

But why Elijah? Why not say that John the Baptist corre-
sponded to some other prophet like Isaiah or Jeremiah? What
made Elijah especially appropriate as a way of describing John the
Baptist's identity? Let's start with some seemingly random observations, from Mark's Gospel and elsewhere, about John the Baptist.
Notice that John confronts a king (Mk. 6:17) and stays in the region of the Jordan (Mt. 3:5; Lk. 3:3) in the wilderness (Mk. 1:4)
across from the Promised Land (Jn. 1:28; 10:40).

Now a few of these details do remind us of Elijah. He too confronted an evil king (1 Kgs. 17:1; 21:17–19) and spent a lot of
time outside of Israel proper (1 Kgs. 17:3, 9). But he also did more.
He called down plagues on the land (1 Kgs. 17:1), called down fire
on his sacrifice (1 Kgs. 18:38), was fed by angels in the wilderness
(1 Kgs. 19:4–7), and met God at Mt. Sinai (1 Kgs. 19:8–14). Elijah
stands out among Old Testament prophets as a new Moses. No one
else was met by God at Mt. Sinai. It is a unique marker in the Bible.
Incidentally, both Moses and Elijah end their careers by ascending—
Moses up a mountain to die and Elijah in a fiery chariot. In both
cases, this happened across the Jordan from Jericho (Deut. 34:1;
2 Kgs. 2:4–8).

There is more to say about John as Elijah, but for now it will suffice to recognize that linking John to Elijah also links him to Moses, the foremost of the prophets.

Yet Moses and all the prophets are about to be surpassed. John is speaking for the whole Mosaic administration when he confesses, "After me One is coming who is mightier than I, and I am not fit to stoop down and untie the thong of His sandals." John's prophecy echoes Malachi's prophecy. Malachi said that a messenger would prepare the way for the Lord; John says that he is preparing the way for Jesus. It is rather hard to escape the idea that Mark is affirming the deity of Jesus by paralleling Malachi's prophecy with John's.

John says the One who is coming will baptize with the Holy Spirit, whereas he merely baptizes with water. It has become something of an American fundamentalist *shibboleth* to use this verse and its parallels to claim that the *real* baptism mentioned in places like Romans 6:3 or Colossians 2:12 is a dry "baptism" done by the Spirit, not with water. Whatever the merits of this idea, it is almost certainly not what John the Baptist was saying, according to Mark and the other Gospel writers. Rather, John refers to the miracle of Pentecost when the Spirit signed and sealed the identity of Jesus' disciples as His new people (Acts 2). After Pentecost and three other Pentecost-like events (Acts 8:14ff; 10:44ff; 19:1ff), water baptism is once again the normal means of entering the Church and gaining access to all the blessings Christ has given the Church (Acts 2:38–41; 22:16).

THE ANOINTING OF JESUS (1:9–11)

Local geo-politics plays a part in the Gospels—though we typically miss it because we don't expect the Bible to teach us about matters that seem so mundane to us. At the time I am writing this chapter I am living between Seattle and Tacoma in the state of Washington. The capital of the state is Olympia, which is a little ways south of Tacoma. Basically, the largest part of the population of the state of Washington is concentrated along the I-5 corridor in western Washington where cities have built up on the shores of the Puget Sound. Thus, if you live on the other side of the mountains in eastern Washington, your impact on the state government is not all that significant. Basically, you are ruled by another region with a very different culture and perhaps even different values. There is very little you can do about it.

Galilee's relationship with Judea was somewhat like that of a small town in eastern Washington to the big cities of western Washington, or perhaps that of Allegheny County to New York City. Jerusalem was the capital of the area; Galilee was at the outskirts. And one prophecy of Christ includes a mention that this area will be exalted:

> There will be no more gloom for her who was in anguish; in earlier times He treated the land of Zebulun and the land of Naphtali with contempt, but later on He shall make it glorious, by the way of the sea, on the other side of Jordan, Galilee of the Gentiles. (Is. 9:1; cf., Mt. 4:15).

Jesus coming from Galilee is in stark contrast to the others coming from Judea and Jerusalem (Mk. 1:5). As "Galilee of the Gentiles" the region had a questionable reputation (cf., Jn. 1:46). Peter Leithart writes:

> The area known as Galilee was part of the land conquered under the leadership of Joshua, and was given to the tribes of Zebulun and Naphtali. In the 8th century B.C., the land was invaded by the Assyrians, many of the inhabitants were taken into exile, and the region was repopulated with Gentiles. Despite an attempt in the second century B.C. to forcibly circumcise and convert the populace, it remained a religiously and ethnically mixed province. It was here that Jesus chose to concentrate at the beginning of His public ministry.[5]

If you are wondering why such geo-politics are in the Bible, you need to remember that at the time there was no secular ideology that separated religion from politics the way it does today. Not only was Jerusalem the political capital of Israel, but it was the religious worship center of the country as well. Proximity to Jerusalem was extremely important since the law of Moses demanded that all Israelites gather at the central sanctuary—the Temple—at the three annual festivals, Passover, Pentecost, and the Feast of Tabernacles.

---

[5] "Galilee of the Gentiles," *Biblical Horizons*, No. 22, February, 1991.

From the very beginning of Israel's history in the land of Canaan, the Israelites who settled west of the Jordan had been suspicious of the faithfulness of their brothers who lived out on the frontier on the other side of that river (Josh. 22). Indeed, human nature being what it is, it would have been far easier for an Israelite in Nazareth (even though it was on the western side of the Jordan) to either neglect or else be legitimately prevented from attending, some of those festivals. Differences in geography represented differences in perceived piety.

Just as the book of Acts records the transfer of the Kingdom from unbelieving Jews to God-fearing Gentiles, so the Gospels record the Kingdom taken from Jerusalem and given to those on the outskirts—geographically, politically, and religiously. Indeed, this shift is not only of importance to the disciples and other contemporaries of Jesus, but is also noticed by the angels of heaven (Acts 1:11).

It is a real irony that the Messiah, the son of David, would come, not from the area associated with the tribe of Judah, but from the land of Naphtali and Zebulun. This was not what Israel expected.

A DOUBLE PORTION OF THE SPIRIT

When Elijah and Elisha had crossed the Jordan River on dry ground, Elijah asked his apprentice what he could do for Elisha before being taken up into heaven. Elisha replied, "please, let a double portion of your spirit be upon me" (2 Kgs. 2:9). There on the western side of the Jordan, Elisha's prayer was heard. He received that double portion, signified by the visibility of Elijah's ascension into heaven and Elijah's discarded cloak left for him to take upon himself. "And he took the mantle of Elijah that fell from him, and struck the waters and said, 'Where is the Lord, the God of Elijah?' And when he also had struck the waters, they were divided here and there; and Elisha crossed over" (2 Kgs. 2:13, 14). He then parted the waters of the Jordan, crossed over to Jericho, and healed that city's cursed water (2 Kgs. 3:19–22).

We have already spoken of some similarities between Elijah and Moses before him. Here is another one: Moses also ascended (albeit to his death) on the west side of the Jordan "opposite Jericho" (Deut. 34:1). He too had a successor, Joshua, who received the Spirit in order to take over where he left off (Deut. 34:9). Furthermore, that successor also crossed the Jordan on dry ground (Josh. 3) and he too went to Jericho (Josh. 5:13ff).

John the Baptist is a new Elijah and Jesus is a new Elisha. John the Baptist is thus a new Moses and Jesus is a new Joshua. From the Jordan River he will execute a "holy war" of sorts for the Kingdom of God. Of course, as the fulfillment of both Joshua and Elisha, the way Jesus wages this war may not be what some expect. Joshua's warfare was straightforward and literal. He went to Jericho and destroyed it. Elisha followed in his footsteps not to destroy, but to save, not to kill, but to make alive. He purified Jericho's water so that the prophets could dwell there. We see dominion being extended, but using remarkably different means. So it will be with Jesus; He will go out conquering and to conquer, yet His battle will not be waged against flesh and blood, but against principality and powers in heavenly places, against spiritual forces of wickedness. Ultimately, He will win the victory paradoxically by letting His enemies destroy Him—a manner of fighting which was unknown both to Joshua and Elisha. He surpasses them both.

A NEW CREATION

At creation, the Spirit fluttered over the chaotic waste that was the first creation (Gen. 1:2). Moses compared the Glory Cloud's hovering over God's people in the wasteland to an eagle hovering over her young (Deut. 32:10, 11). He used the same word to describe the eagle's flight that he used earlier to describe the Spirit's activity over creation. He also used the same word to describe the wilderness that he used to describe the unformed watery earth. These are the only two places in the entire Pentateuch where those words are used, and they are used together both times. Moses was telling the Israelites that God's leading them through the wilderness in that glorious fiery cloud was reminiscent of the creation of the world when the Spirit brought order and life from the wilderness of the primal world.

But the Spirit doesn't descend on Jesus in the form of an eagle.

Why a dove? Perhaps the most prominent dove in the Hebrew Scriptures was the one sent by Noah to look for dry ground after the flood (Gen. 8:7–12). What does this dove have to do with the Spirit? A great deal. After all, the original creation was a great water and the Spirit brought new life from it. When God decided to destroy humanity, He reduced the world once again to a watery mass. Noah sent his dove out over the face of the deep to find new life, and it brought back to him the first fruit of a new creation.

And now a dove once again is seen hovering over the waters, the Spirit over a new creation. All of Paul's theology of Jesus as the second Adam (1 Cor. 15:20ff) may have come from reflecting on this event. "For neither is circumcision anything, nor uncircumcision," he later wrote, "but a new creation." Mark agrees. John's ministry meant that the old Israel had failed and needed to be reborn. But only in Jesus can this new creation come to life. The Spirit hovering over the waters is the sign and seal of His new vocation.

We have seen in Jesus a fulfillment of Joshua's reception of the Spirit and His installation as the leader of God's people. We have seen in Jesus a fulfillment of Elisha's double portion of the Spirit from Elijah and his healing ministry. But we must not forget that Jesus is the Christ, the anointed king of Israel. His identity cannot be covered by the prophets nor by the priesthood. He is more than a judge under the Mosaic era (Joshua–Judges). He is a Davidic king. The Voice from heaven announces at His baptism that Jesus is His son just as that same voice told His forefather David, "I will be a father to him and he will be a son to Me" (2 Sam. 7:14). The Apostle Paul will later write a theology of baptism for the (new, re-created) people of God that builds on this unique baptism:

> For you are all *sons of God* through faith in Christ Jesus. *For all of you* who *were baptized into Christ* have clothed yourselves with Christ. There is neither Jew nor Greek, there is neither slave nor free man, there is neither male nor female; for you are all one in Christ Jesus. And if you belong to Christ, then you are Abraham's offspring, heirs according to promise. (Gal. 3:26–29; emphasis added)

Jesus is baptized and is declared God's Son. We are baptized and, even though no audible word is spoken from heaven, the act has been forever interpreted by what happened to Jesus. We who are baptized have therein too been pronounced as God's sons and daughters. In his anointing we too have been anointed (2 Cor. 1:21), and we are kings with him (Rev. 1:6; 5:10; 1 Pet. 2:9). Our baptism is our call to royal office.

Incidentally, though the call of the Spirit through the sign of baptism is important, it ultimately points to something in the future. The Spirit who anointed Jesus for the task ahead of Him by coming upon Him in the Jordan River, will fulfill that task through Him by raising Jesus from the dead—and eventually raising all of us as well (Rom. 8:11). Just as Jesus was "pronounced the Son of God . . . by the resurrection of the dead through the Spirit of Holiness," so we will be adopted as sons and daughters of God when the Spirit raises us to a glorious new life (Rom. 8:23). Baptism is a sign and seal of our royal sonship, partly because it anticipates what will be bestowed on us at the resurrection.

All this has implications that are less than attractive to most people. By anointing Jesus to claim His throne, the Spirit was anointing Him to die. And it is all the more true of us:

> The Spirit Himself bears witness with our spirit that we are children of God, and if children, heirs also, heirs of God and fellow heirs with Christ, *if indeed we suffer with Him in order that we may also be glorified with Him.* (Rom. 8:16, 17; emphasis added)

Jesus' contemporaries will later hear him speak of the cross and their need to take up the cross, and they will not understand it. They had a different job description for a king.

Do we?

THE TESTING OF JESUS (1:12–14)

Mark is writing the final story of the great story and stories of the Bible. The story of the exodus from the old world in Egypt and the trials in the wilderness for the people of God is an obvious theme throughout the New Testament, and it is certainly present in his Gospel. The Israelites were led by a pillar of fire and cloud which was the same Spirit of God that had hovered over creation. Jesus was overshadowed by the Spirit in the form of a dove and led into the wilderness by that same Spirit. The Israelites were also led into the wilderness and there fed on manna, the bread of angels (Ps. 78:25), and were given the Law by angels (Heb. 2:2).

Yet unlike Matthew and Luke, Mark does not bother to record the three specific temptations. Instead, he gives us a brief detail that the others leave out: "He was with the wild beasts." What is Mark trying to get across by including this detail? Given the strong royal theme and the Solomonic wisdom to which he has alluded, the reader may consider David's testimony as to how God trained him to prepare him for Goliath:

> But David said to Saul, "Your servant was tending his father's sheep. When a lion or a bear came and took a lamb from the flock, I went out after him and attacked him, and rescued it from his mouth; and when he rose up against me, I seized him by his beard and struck him and killed him. Your servant has killed both the lion and the bear; and this uncircumcised Philistine will be like one of them, since he has taunted the armies of the living God." And David said, "The Lord who delivered me from the paw of the lion and from the paw of the bear, He will deliver me from the hand of this Philistine." (1 Sam. 17:34–37)

When Samuel anointed Saul we read that "the Spirit of the Lord came mightily upon David from that day forward" (1 Sam. 16:13). In addition to Moses and Joshua, Elijah and Elisha, we find John the Baptist and Jesus have fulfilled the roles of Samuel and David. Matthew and Luke both bring out the first two associations, but Mark seems unique in alluding to the last one in the wilderness temptations (and by implication in his baptism). He will emphasize it even more in just a few sentences.

PREACHING THE GOOD NEWS (1:14, 15)

Mark closes this first section of his work with the results of Jesus' anointing and training: Jesus preaches the gospel. This represents a jump in time, as we discover from John's record. But Mark is uninterested in that early period after Jesus' baptism. Rather he cuts to a point in time when Jesus' ministry reached an intensified level. Jesus' predecessor had now been taken away into prison by Herod.

God destroyed Pharaoh through Moses, and Elijah received

God's divine protection from Ahab, but God allows John to be imprisoned by Pharaoh's and Ahab's successor. This gives us a clue that, though Joshua defeated the Canaanites, and Elisha died in his bed, Jesus may not be spared from His enemies.

Jesus is about to call His first four disciples to follow Him on His mission. Mark deliberately associates this with the passing of John from the scene. Later, when Jesus sends His disciples out on a mission, Mark will choose that place to tell us that John has passed even further from the scene, from Herod's guards to his executioner (Mk. 6). He is stressing to us that Jesus was John's successor and that His ministry became prominent as John's ceased.

Mark summarizes Jesus' message thus: "The time is fulfilled, and the kingdom of God is at hand; repent and believe in the gospel" (Mk. 1:15). The original hearers unquestionably would have heard in this message a promise of imminent deliverance for God's people and a challenge to trust the messenger. And if the message was true, then that meant God was drawing near. Repentance would be the only rational option.

Mark leaves much of the content of Jesus' message to other writers (What is the Kingdom of God like? What should people repent of?). But one can't help noticing that Jesus' gospel centers on himself. John spoke of One who would come after him. Jesus now says the time has arrived. Plainly Jesus Himself is somehow integrally related to the dawning of the Kingdom.

Jesus was called not only to serve but to be the Kingdom. Soon we will see that He calls others likewise. Though the crisis time of Jesus' earthly work is now over, still He calls.

Mark 1:16–2:13

Calling & Restoration

Mark's Gospel has begun with a flurry of activity: introduction, prophecy, John's ministry, John's prophecy, Jesus' baptism, Jesus' testing, Jesus' ministry. Now things start to slow down slightly. Mark begins to give us larger literary units devoted to the events he wishes to relate to us.

A NEW VOCATION (1:16–20)

In 1 Kings 19:19–21, we read that Elijah the prophet found Elisha while he was plowing with a pair of oxen. Elijah threw his cloak upon him. In response, Elisha got permission from Elijah to first kiss his father and mother good-bye and then slaughtered the oxen and cooked them by burning the harness and other implements. Having given those around a feast, he then left to serve Elijah.

We have stated that Jesus was a new Elisha as the successor of John the Baptist, the new Elijah. But we must not forget that Elisha was recognized as being a new Elijah himself, having inherited his spiritual power and ministry (2 Kgs. 2:15). It should not surprise us if we see Jesus, as a new Elisha, acting as a greater Elijah as well. And here we see Him, like Elijah before Him, calling His successors from their (former) vocations as fishermen and telling them to follow him. Jesus' call has more urgency. Mark gives us no sign of Simon, Andrew, James, and John even speaking to their parents, let alone hosting a feast (the feasting must wait until after they have begun following Jesus).

In Jesus' call of His first four disciples, we see Him acting as one who is filled with the Spirit and thus is fulfilling the role of the Spirit. In verse 10 we saw the Spirit descend upon Jesus as He came up from the banks of the Jordan. That same Spirit then drove him into the wilderness to be trained. The Spirit, in a word, called Jesus. Now, Jesus, filled with the Holy Spirit, is the one who calls the disciples. They too are called from the shallows of the sea.

Of course, the fact that fishermen are called from their occupation and from water might strike us as simply a coincidence. If Jesus wants to call fishermen in the midst of their work, it would be hard not to call them in the context of water. Yet, when Jesus calls Levi from his money table to leave his vocation and follow him, we find Mark making sure to let us know that this too happened by the seashore (2:13–14). And then when Jesus selects the Twelve, even though they are on a mountain, Mark makes sure we know that this mountain is by the sea and that Jesus took the twelve up from the sea to ordain them to their new office (3:7, 13). There are many details which, in our curiosity, we could wish Mark had included in his account, but which he does not. The fact that he insists on revealing this one should give us pause.

The new creation is spreading. Just as the Spirit hovering over Jesus as He comes up from the waters hearkens back to Genesis 1:2, so we see now that the new creation continues with Jesus calling others from the water as Himself a life-giving Spirit.

Parenthetically, we can see how Mark reveals the full gospel story despite his compact brevity. When Elijah called Elisha by throwing his cloak over him, that was only the beginning. Eventually, Elisha would see his master taken up into the Heavens. He would, before this occurred, have the boldness to ask for a double portion of the Spirit that had empowered Elijah. That God had granted his request would be signified by his witnessing Elijah's ascent in the fiery angelic chariot. Elisha went on to do greater miracles than his master had done (2 Kgs. 2:7–14).

And so we can know, even though Mark stops his account much earlier, that these chosen disciples who have been called to serve Jesus will eventually be their Master's heirs and successors. They too will see their Master taken from them into heaven. They too will be granted a greater portion of the Spirit to do greater miracles. They too will have this signified to them by the visible mark of fire from heaven. Let the reader understand.

SOOTHING SAUL (1:21–28)

After Jesus was called, He was led into the wilderness to be trained and to do combat with Satan. It seems jarring, therefore, that after the disciples are called, he does not take them to the wilderness, but to the synagogue. But—surprise, surprise—the synagogue doesn't turn out to be such an incongruous place for fighting the spiritual enemy after all! Just as Jesus was victorious in his trials with Satan, so here He will be confronted by one of Satan's underlings and will triumph.

Was it some sort of anomaly that an unclean spirit would possesses a man in the synagogue or manifest himself in a synagogue? Mark indicates otherwise in verse 38: "And He went into their synagogues throughout all Galilee, preaching and casting out the demons." Common sense may tell the reader that the casting out of demons simply happened during these trips as Jesus went to synagogues to preach in them. But the grammar lends itself to the interpretation that Jesus went to the synagogues as much to exorcize them as to preach in them.

Even the demon's reaction to Jesus puts the synagogue in a bad light: "Have you come to destroy *us*? I know who You are—the Holy One of God!" (Emphasis added) Does the demon perceive Jesus as a threat to the entire synagogue? True, several chapters later we will run into the possibility that a demon-possessed man can be held by many demons at once. But this demon speaks of himself in the singular in the very next sentence; he does not say "We know who You are," but rather, "I know who You are." To all appearances, the demon is worried that Jesus will destroy the synagogue.

Jesus, nevertheless, cleanses the man of the unclean Spirit to the amazement of the rest of the people in the synagogue. His gag order to the demon that he not say who He is seems designed to avoid a confrontation. He will do this again with the leper (vv. 40–45) with less success, and then give up on avoiding conflict when the paralytic is brought to him (2:1–12). Finally, He will evoke a murderous rage in the synagogue and be forced to flee the area and regroup (3:1–8ff).

In the way Mark portrays this conflict, we see Jesus as a greater

David once again with the synagogue system shown to us as a worse King Saul. Unlike Matthew, only Mark places an exorcism as Christ's first miracle in close proximity to Jesus' own anointing by the Holy Spirit at his baptism. This follows the story of David's own anointing by Samuel the prophet and by God's Spirit. We read:

> Then Samuel took the horn of oil and anointed him in the midst of his brothers; and the Spirit of the LORD came mightily upon David from that day forward . . . Now the Spirit of the LORD departed from Saul, and an evil spirit from the LORD terrorized him . . . And Saul sent to Jesse, saying, "Let David now stand before me; for he has found favor in my sight." So it came about whenever the evil spirit from God came to Saul, David would take the harp and play it with his hand; and Saul would be refreshed and be well, and the evil spirit would depart from him. (1 Sam. 16:13–14; 22–23)

The parallels are hard to miss: Both David and Jesus are filled with the Spirit through the action of another (Samuel anointing and John baptizing). Both then find an evil spirit tormenting another person and both are able to do something about it. Mark alone arranges for this exorcism to fall so near after the story of the Spirit coming upon Jesus. Again, we see Jesus is a greater David. He speaks with authority, even authority over the unclean spirits.

MUTING THE DEMONS

Mark's Gospel is commonly cited as the one among the four that deals the most with "the messianic secret." Unbelievers use this observation to theorize that Jesus never claimed to be the Messiah. Mark is alleged to be the earliest Gospel and thus was forced to face up to the fact that Jesus never made any messianic claim. Mark thus made up the idea that Jesus only secretly told a few followers that he was the Messiah.

The problem with this whole scheme is that it presupposes that the Scripture is merely a book without divine authority and that we are free to disbelieve its account of itself and come up with alternative hypotheses. For those who are inclined to worship and serve their own imaginations in this way, an appeal to God's authority and His inspiration of the text is meaningless; all that matters is the latest issues of speculations which are proffered as an alternative to the Gospels' own explanation as to why and how they were written.

Since this is not a work of apologetics, I will only offer one observation to those enamored by such imaginings: It is simply incredible that a popular teacher and leader in first century Palestine would *not* make any messianic claim. Are we to believe that Josephus' portrayals of leaders claiming to be the Messiah were all fictional? More pointedly, are we to believe that in a book obviously intended to vindicate Christianity, Luke would make up the fact that the early Church was twice compared to militaristic liberation movements (Acts 5:36, 37), once mistaken for a terrorist group (Acts 21:38), and once accused of sedition (Acts 17:7)? Plainly, Jesus claimed to be king.

Mark's Gospel is perhaps the one most interested in showing forth Jesus' kingship. While all of the Gospels are unanimous in proclaiming that Jesus is the heir of David and the promised king of Israel, Mark seems to have a special interest in relating Jesus to the kingdom period in Israel's history. So far we have seen Mark alone associating wild beasts with Jesus' trials in the wilderness. Mark alone has a Davidic contrast between the Holy Spirit anointing Jesus to enable him to deal with the demonic spirits haunting the synagogues of Israel. Indeed, Mark alone begins with a reference to "beginning" or "first principle," and then an expounding of "the way of the Lord" in line with the Solomonic wisdom in Proverbs addressed to the son.

When David challenged Goliath, he did not reveal to Saul that he had been anointed as Israel's new king and thus had God's promise of personal safety and victory in dealing with the giant. He kept that piece of information to himself. David, to use the language of modern thought, had a "messianic secret." By emphasizing that aspect of Jesus' ministry, Mark is strengthening yet another tie with David and kingship.

THE AUTHORITY OF THE NEW

Mark tells us (Mk. 1:22) that Jesus didn't teach as the scribes did, but rather as one with authority. Then, in response to Jesus' miracle, the congregation of the synagogue exclaims, "What is this? A new teaching with authority! He commands even the unclean spirits, and they obey Him!" It would be easy to interpret this authority as a reference to Jesus' deity, and that may be part of the truth. But the people recognize that it is not simply that Jesus possesses authority that makes His teaching distinctive. Rather they observe that His *new* teaching carries new authority. Jesus is God but Jesus is also a new man, called by the Father and anointed by the Spirit to bring a new age. As Jesus will later explain in the face of opposition:

> No one sews a patch of unshrunk cloth on an old garment; otherwise the patch pulls away from it, the new from the old, and a worse tear results. And no one puts new wine into old wineskins; otherwise the wine will burst the skins, and the wine is lost, and the skins as well; but one puts new wine into fresh wineskins. (Mk. 2:22–23)

Jesus' teaching, remember, is that the Kingdom is at hand and the time is fulfilled (Mk. 1:15). Scribes repeating ordinances meant for a dying age must learn a new message or else die with them. Right now, the crowd is merely amazed, and Jesus mutes the demon to ensure that hostilities do not break out.

But soon there will be no way to avoid conflict.

RAISED UP TO SERVE (1:29–39)

Jesus' four disciples dropped out of view in the story of the synagogue. Now they are suddenly named again. In Simon's house we come to the second of Jesus' healing miracles in Mark's Gospel. This time, instead of an exorcism Mark shows us a restoration. Simon's mother-in-law is unable to walk or function due to a fever. Jesus *raises her up*. This is the language of most of Jesus' restorations. It is the language of resurrection (cf., Mk. 5:41; 6:14, 16; 14:28; 16:6), but Mark finds a way of working it into most of his accounts of restorations. Not only does Jesus "raise" many up, but even those who are not unable to stand nevertheless are found seated and need to be told to "arise" (3:3; 10:49).

But raised for what purpose? Jesus restores His people to service. As soon as He heals Simon's mother-in-law, she serves them at table. We will see this pattern unfold further as Mark progresses.

HUNTED

There is an odd aftermath to this miracle and meal. First, Jesus is mobbed by people seeking healing. This is not surprising. What is surprising is that Mark does not describe this sudden fame in positive terms. Jesus heals and exorcises, and then He sneaks off into the night. The reason for His leaving is innocent enough: He wants to pray. Yet His disciples *hunt Him down* (Mk. 1:36). Mark chooses a word used in the Greek translation of the Hebrew Scriptures to describe Saul's pursuit of David (1 Sam. 23:25). Indeed, it is only used in the Old Testament to describe hostile pursuit.[1] For the Biblically literate Greek reader, this would give a malevolent tone to Simon's report, "Everyone is looking for You" (v. 37).

Why such a negative portrayal of Jesus' popularity? Mark gives us no answer yet, but as we see how even favorable crowds are able to harass Jesus and how they also draw unfavorable attention upon him, it will seem quite appropriate to say that Jesus is hunted down by everyone.

Jesus' response is to leave the area. As far as we can tell from Mark, He never even goes back into town.

CLEANSING & CONTAMINATED (1:40–45)

Mark shows us Jesus summoning Peter, Andrew, James, and John and afterwards casting out an "unclean spirit" in the synagogue. Then Mark mentions them all again in Simon's house restoring his mother-in-law to service, and now he shows us a leper being cleansed. Thus far we see a repeated twofold pattern.

---

[1] The relevant passages in Scripture are: Genesis 14:14; Exodus 14:8; Joshua 8:17; Judges 9:40; 1 Samuel 23:25; 30:10; 2 Samuel 2:19, 24; 1 Kings 20:20; 2 Chronicles 13:19; 14:12; Psalm 108:16; 142:3; Jeremiah 52:8; Lamentations 3:11. From the Apocrypha: 1 Maccabees 10:78; 12:30; 16:9; Baruch 4:25.

a1   Jesus is called to service at baptism (1:9–11).
b1   Jesus calls Peter, Andrew, James, & John to service(1:16–20).
c1   Jesus with Peter, Andrew, James, & John restore Simon's
         mother-in-law to service (1:29–39).
a2   Jesus combats Satan in the wilderness (1:12–15).
b2   Jesus combats unclean spirit in synagogue (1:21–28).
c2   Jesus cleanses a leper in the wilderness (1:40–45).

What has cleansing a leper to do with casting out a demon? Much in every way as far as Mark is concerned. In the first place, Mark refers to the demon as an "unclean spirit."[2] Exorcism is thus portrayed as a sort of cleansing. In the second place, just as Jesus silenced the demon to keep him from revealing his identity, so he now (with less success!) tries to get the cleansed leper to keep quiet. Thirdly, though the exorcism took place in a synagogue, not the desert, what Jesus does involves something greater than the synagogue system: the Temple itself. Jesus instructs the man to go to the priests as the Law of Moses directed. Finally, Jesus' new authority accompanying His new teaching results in a potential conflict, not with the scribes, but with the priesthood. Cleansing for leprosy was given into their hands (Lev. 14:1), yet Jesus, who is not even of the tribe of Levi, does a quicker and better job than they could.

I should mention that modern leprosy has nothing to do with leprosy in the Bible. In the Scriptures leprosy was a discoloration of the skin or clothing or the walls of a house (Lev. 13, 14).[3] The problem with getting Biblical leprosy was simply that it rendered one unclean. This meant one couldn't approach the Tabernacle or Temple and one couldn't live in populated areas. Leprosy, like all ceremonial uncleanness, caused exile from God's special presence. By cleansing the leper, Jesus was granting him access to God's sanctuary. Now he could attend Passover and the other feasts in Jerusalem. Now he could live in a town.

---

[2] The basis for this analogy between demons inhabiting a person and uncleanness may be located in Leviticus 11:29–35. There, if a swarming thing gets into a vessel or oven the vessel or oven, must be smashed because it has become unclean and will only issue uncleanness. Jesus, however, is able to extract the unclean spirit from the clay vessels of humanity without breaking them apart.

[3] Many translations use different words for what it is that afflicts one's skin, clothing, or house. But the Bible uses only one word for all three situations.

We will see many times when Jesus combats uncleanness, either by driving out an unclean spirit or by cleansing a woman with an issue of blood. In all of those cases, Jesus demonstrates authority and an inability to become unclean Himself. This case is slightly different. Jesus touches the leper and then, as a result of the cleansed leper's disobedience to His command, ends up suffering the fate of a leper. Jesus must now remain in unpopulated areas and never publicly enter cities. Though He is clean He suffers as if unclean because He touched one who was unclean and made him clean. It is hard to imagine a more vivid picture of Jesus suffering under the curse that those who deserved the curse might experience a blessing.

THE AUTHORITY OF THE SON OF MAN (2:1–13)

Conflict was inevitable.

Jesus avoided it when He placed a gag order on the demon. He tried to avoid it when He cleansed the leper by telling him to go submit to the priests, lawful authorities who had jurisdiction over such matters. He evaded conflict for a while by staying in rural regions. But now He has returned to His new home, and He knows that a showdown is unavoidable.

Mark writes that Jesus was "at home" (v. 1). But Capernaum was not where Jesus was from, nor where His family lived. Rather, Capernaum was Simon Peter's home. Jesus does not announce His repudiation of the natural family in favor of a new family until later (3:31–35), but Mark reveals to us that already Jesus is founding a new household around Himself. It is temporarily headquartered, it seems, in Simon's house. Jesus, as He teaches the crowds, is sitting in the nucleus of the first Church.

BURIAL

In 2 Kings 13:20 we read:

> And Elisha died, and they buried him. Now the bands of the Moabites would invade the land in the spring of the year. And as they were burying a man, behold, they saw a marauding band; and they cast the man into the grave of Elisha. And when the man touched the bones of Elisha, he revived and stood up on his feet.

So it happens again here. We have four men carrying one who cannot move. They dig a hole (Mk. 2:4) and lower the man down into it. Having been lowered down to where Jesus was, the man is suddenly able to stand on his feet. Jesus tells him to *rise up*. Here again we see restoration presented as resurrection.

FAITH

Jesus first declares that the man's sins have been forgiven and does so because He sees the faith of the four friends (v. 5). People who spend a lot of time reading systematic theologians start scratching their heads about this statement. "How can someone be justified by someone else's faith?" Or, if Jesus saw the faith of all five persons, "How can one individual's justification be through the faith of other persons in addition to his own?"

One might as well ask how faith became a visible quality in the presence of Jesus and what its color was. Jesus saw the faith of the four men and was moved by it *because He saw their concrete actions*. He saw their faith in the fact that they willingly carried their friend to Him and surpassed many obstacles to get Him there. If one wants conclusions from this for a list in a theology textbook, then perhaps we can glean that faith implies hope for what God will do. And if conditions are placed on the promises of God for the future, then faith is the name for the motive that prompts a person to meet those conditions. In this case, the future hope was that Jesus would heal their friend and the condition was that he be brought to Jesus' attention.

In response, Jesus forgives the man's sins by what is called a "performative utterance." Like a pastor at the climax of a wedding ceremony saying, "I now pronounce you husband and wife," Jesus adopts and forgives this man: "My child, your sins are forgiven." We commonly think of God the Father as the one who adopts us, but Jesus is the new Adam and is thus the forefather of all who are forgiven. Again we see Jesus remaking a family centered around Himself.

We need to remind ourselves about the meaning of forgiveness in Mark's Gospel, which we reviewed in chapter one. Forgiveness not only had a personal application, but a national or corporate fulfillment as well. Forgiveness meant a return from exile—an ending of the curse. On the personal level, this may explain why Jesus told the paralytic that he was His child and was forgiven. The paralytic has by far the most serious of the illnesses we have yet encountered. Quite possibly the man believed that God was punishing him for his sins or perhaps for the sins of his parents (cf., Jn. 9:1).

Christians typically do not think much about the fact that we claim to have received God's pardon for our sins and yet suffer as much as our unbelieving neighbors. Our children get injured or killed in automobile accidents, our parents get Alzheimer's, and our wives get breast cancer while our husbands are afflicted in the prostate. All around us we see the effects of the curse for sin demolishing our world, Christian and non-Christian alike. And yet we boldly claim to have been forgiven.

Imagine a man sitting in a prison cell contemplating a lifelong prison sentence. How overjoyed he would be if he received news that the President had issued a pardon for all his crimes! But wait. What if he jumped up and tried to leave the prison, only to find the cell door slammed in his face. What happened? *The President forgave you*, he is told, *but he has not overturned your sentence. You are no longer to be considered guilty of the crime, but you must remain behind bars.* Wouldn't this be considered a rather paltry form of forgiveness?

So it is not unnatural that people find it difficult to believe their sins have been forgiven when they find themselves suffering as much from the effects of God's wrath on sinful humanity as do the ungodly. And this difficulty is the bone of contention in Jesus' ministry and is that of the subsequent Church of the New Testament. Israel was hoping for deliverance from their enemies and the curse. Jesus comes claiming that deliverance is at hand, and yet Rome continues to oppress them, Herod remains in power, and a corrupt priesthood still rules in Jerusalem. How can the kingdom have come—how can their sins have been forgiven—with such darkness still afflicting God's people? And how can the Church declare that the new age has dawned if death remains unchecked, and poverty, slavery, wife-abuse, disease, and other evils continue as if nothing has happened?

Jesus' answer is that His Word should assure them of their for-giveness and that it should make them certain of a future hope based on God's new relationship with them. The pardon is real and the stay in prison will not last forever, though there may be redemptive reasons why God has not yet accomplished an imme-diate release. But when some doubt Jesus' word and even think that He blasphemes, Jesus gives a token sign that He is to be trusted. "Which is easier, to say to the paralytic, 'Your sins are forgiven'; or to say, 'Arise, and take up your pallet and walk'?" The paralytic will still die at the end of his natural life. He is still under the curse as we all are. But any thought that he has been *especially* cursed by God has now been reversed with a special intervention indicating that he is especially loved by God.

A NEW PLACE OF GRACE

The scribes and Pharisees knew that sins could be forgiven. In-deed, they even knew that men who had received such authority from God could bestow such forgiveness. Leviticus is quite clear: "So the priest shall make atonement on his behalf for his sin which he has committed, and it shall be forgiven him" (Lev. 5:10). But Jesus is neither a priest, nor at the altar in the forecourt of the Temple, nor offering blood there on behalf of the one seeking for-giveness. Far away from Jerusalem and the Temple, without any ancestry in the tribe of Levi and lacking any sacrificial blood to display to God, Jesus forgave the paralytic's sins by merely a word.

Jesus offered true liberation. Slaughtering animals for the for-giveness of sins must have been economic bondage for the Israel-ites. Doing so in Capernaum meant that a region far from a central sanctuary had suddenly been brought near to God. This should have prompted much rejoicing. For some it did (Mk. 2:12).

But some did not rejoice. The scribes and the Pharisees saw that Jesus was overturning the old order, the order given to them by Moses. No benefit could compensate for threatening their way of life. They would be watching Jesus closely.

THE NEW ADAM & ISRAEL EMBODIED

On what basis could Jesus explain why the order established through Moses on the pillars of Priesthood, Sanctuary, Sacrifice, and Law (which explained the other three) would be set aside by God and replaced by another authority? The only hint of an explanation is the title Jesus ascribed to Himself, "the Son of Man," which he claimed possessed "authority on earth" to forgive (Mk. 2:10).

Following Austin Farrer, I think we have here a reference to the vision of "one like a Son of Man" in Daniel 7, as is especially clear if we take into account the popular Greek translation of the Hebrew Scriptures.

> "The Son of Man hath authority upon earth" puts together the most important phrases of Daniel 7. "There came as *a Son of Man* ... and there was given him *authority* and all the nations *of the earth* after their families and all glory serving him; his *authority* is an everlasting *authority* that shall not be taken away, and his kingdom that shall not be destroyed." ... We need to take into account two other features of Daniel 7. With one we are already familiar: the equation drawn between the authority of God and the authority of the Son of Man, or of the Saints, on this earth. The other is Daniel's own paraphrase of his vision which he makes in recapitulating it. Where the vision says, "There came as a Son of Man ... and authority was given to him," the recapitulation says, "He (God) gave *judgment* to the Saints of the Most High" (7:22) ... Putting Daniel's several statements together, we get the result: the divine authority over the earth, and especially the divine authority in judgment, is given to the Son of Man. Now if the divine authority of judgment does not consist in the remitting and retaining of sins, in what does it consist? The Pharisees say that God reserves this power; but Daniel says he confers it on the Son of Man.[4]

The New American Standard Version translates Daniel 7:22 as "judgment was passed in favor of the saints," but its margin reading is "judgment was given for the saints." In Revelation 20:4 the scene from Daniel is revisited:

> And I saw thrones, and they sat upon them, and judgment was given to them. And I saw the souls of those who had been beheaded because of the testimony of Jesus and because of the word

[4] *A Study in Saint Mark* (New York, Oxford Univ. Press, 1952), 271ff.

of God, and those who had not worshiped the beast or his image, and had not received the mark upon their forehead and upon their hand; and they came to life and reigned with Christ for a thousand years.

The testimony of John's vision, then, is that not only is judgment passed in favor of the saints, but the power of judgment is transferred to the saints and they reign with that new authority.

But we cannot rest with an authority given to the Son of Man in Daniel, unless we also discuss how Jesus is identifying that Son of Man with Himself. Those of us raised in evangelical homes are used to thinking that Daniel's vision of the Son of Man is a vision of Jesus with a straight one-to-one correspondence between the one in the vision and Jesus.

That is the correct result, but the proper path to get there is somewhat more complicated. Unquestionably, Daniel understood his vision to be not about a single future individual, but about "the saints," the faithful remnant of Israel. This is inescapable given the fact that Daniel 7 contains an explanation of his vision of one like a Son of Man being given world dominion and bringing about the destruction of ravenous beasts. This explanation states quite clearly that "the Son of Man" being given authority represents the promise that "the sovereignty, the dominion, and the greatness of all the kingdoms under the whole heaven will be given to the people of the saints of the Highest One; His kingdom will be an everlasting kingdom, and all the dominions will serve and obey Him" (Dan. 7:27). Furthermore, in the vision of Daniel 7, the appearance of the Son of Man is preceded by the appearance of four great beasts representing four great empires. If the beasts do not denote specific individuals, but rather various empires, why should Daniel expect the Son of Man to be an individual rather than a collective group?

Furthermore, the imagery of a Son of Man has Biblical precedent. According to Psalm 80, Israel is "the Son of Man."

You removed a vine from Egypt;
You drove out the nations, and planted it.
You cleared the ground before it,
And it took deep root and filled the land.

The mountains were covered with its shadow;
And the cedars of God with its boughs.
It was sending out its branches to the sea,
And its shoots to the River.
Why have You broken down its hedges,
So that all who pass that way pick its fruit?
A boar from the forest eats it away,
And whatever moves in the field feeds on it.
O God of hosts, turn again now, we beseech You;
Look down from heaven and see, and take care of this vine,
Even the shoot which Your right hand has planted,
And on the son whom You hath strengthened for Yourself.
It is burned with fire, it is cut down;
They perish at the rebuke of Your countenance.
Let Your hand be upon the man of Your right hand,
Upon the son of man whom You made strong for Yourself. (vv. 8 –17)

This Psalm provides an excellent basis for the vision of Daniel 7, with its theme of foreign invasion and the four beasts from the sea playing the part of the "boar from the forest." But why would the Psalmist use the term "son of man"? If we bear in mind that the Hebrew could also be translated "son of Adam," then the vision of Daniel 7 can provide us an answer. Daniel 7 shows us four beasts followed by a son of Adam who is given dominion over them. The reference to the sixth day of Creation is unmistakable.

Plainly then, a "son of Adam" is a new Adam, given his worldwide, or perhaps even greater, dominion. This new Adam is defined as Israel by Psalm 80 and as the saints of the Most High by Daniel 7. The basis for this identity goes back to Genesis where only three people are told to "be fruitful and multiply." The first command is given to Adam with the original dominion mandate (Gen. 1:28) and then, understandably, to Noah, when God makes a covenant with him after the flood (Gen. 9:1, 7). So far we're merely following the NASB study notes. But someone else is also told to "be fruitful and multiply": Jacob (Gen. 35:11). Indeed, Jacob follows God's instructions and propagates twelve sons. Two generations before him, Abraham also heard those words in God's covenant with him, not given as command but as a promise of divine action.

Now when Abram was ninety-nine years old, the LORD appeared to Abram and said to him,

"I am God Almighty;
Walk before Me, and be blameless.
And I will establish My covenant between Me and you,
And *I will multiply you exceedingly*."
And Abram fell on his face, and God talked with him, saying,
"As for Me, behold, My covenant is with you,
And you shall be the father of a multitude of nations.
No longer shall your name be called Abram,
But your name shall be Abraham;
For I will make you the father of a multitude of nations.
And *I will make you exceedingly fruitful* . . .". (Gen. 17:1–6a; emphasis added)

The lesson of Genesis in all this is that Israel is God's new humanity. It is quite proper to refer to that kingdom as a "Son of Adam" and compare its foreign oppressors to a boar of the forest or to beasts from the sea.

But then why does Jesus take to Himself the title of the Son of Adam? In one sense, that question is answered by following the events in Mark's Gospel. Only as Israel is faithful while being tormented by the beasts can she claim to be God's new humanity. Jesus alone will remain faithful, and the calling of Israel will narrow down to Him alone.

But we must not forget another explanation: The King represents and even embodies His people. As the Christ, the Lord, and the Son of God (Mk. 1:1), Jesus represents Israel. Just as David's unfaithfulness brought God's wrath on Israel (1 Chr. 21), so Jesus' faithfulness will bring blessing upon the Israel of God. Ultimately Jesus' unique claim to be the Son of Man does not undermine Daniel's interpretation, but undergirds it. Precisely *because* Jesus is the Son of Man, the saints will also be given judgment and a kingdom, just as Revelation 20:4 portrays. We are God's new humanity as believers because the one in whom we trust is ultimately God's New Human. "For even as the body is one and yet has many members," writes the Apostle Paul, "and all the members of the body, though they are many, are one body, so also is Christ" (1 Cor. 12:13). Christ is a royal title, and we as the subjects of King Jesus are found in Him and are counted as Him. He is the Son of Adam, and therefore so are we.

Thus, the power to forgive sins is no longer restricted as it once was. If Jesus has such authority as the Son of Man then so do all who are found in Him. Matthew says this explicitly in his recounting of the healing of the paralytic: "And when the multitudes saw this, they were filled with awe, and glorified God, who had given such authority to men" (Mt. 9:8). Matthew then goes on to explain how this new power is transferred from Christ to others (Mt. 16:19; 18:18), as does the Apostle John (Jn. 20:23). Mark, in keeping with his cryptic style, leaves us to figure it out without his help. The results are clear. Time and again the saints are exhorted to forgive one another (Gal. 6:1; Eph. 4:32; Col. 3:13; Jas. 5:15, 19–20), an exhortation for which there is very little precedent in the Hebrew Scriptures. We have been given judgment.

CONCLUSION

We have covered several stories now in chapters 1 and 2 of Mark's Gospel. Before we move on to a new section, perhaps we should ask ourselves if there is any method to Mark. I've already mentioned some patterns of calling/restoration followed by conflict with uncleanness. That rhythm actually begins with the first verses of Mark, as Austin Farrer has observed. His table is reproduced here with minor alterations:

* ❋   Gospel prophecies (1:1–3)
* ◆   John's baptism (1:4–5)
* ❋   John's desert life and prophecy (1:6–8)
* ◆   Christ baptized and called (1:9–11)
* ❋   Christ's desert conflict with Satan (1:12–13)
* ◆   Christ's call of Simon and Co. (1:14–20)
* ❋   Christ casts out an unclean spirit (1:21–28)
* ◆   Christ raises up Simon's mother-in-law in Simon's house (1:29–39)

✱ Christ cleanses an unclean leper (1:40–45)

◆ Christ raises up a paralytic in Simon's house (2:1–11)[5]

So now our section ends with Jesus once again at the seashore preaching His Gospel (Mk. 2:13). How do we know that this counts as the end of a section? We began with Jesus' calling of the four disciples, Peter, Andrew, James, and John from the midst of their vocation. Now He will soon call another to abandon his secular labor and follow Him. Just before He calls the disciples, we read, "And after John had been taken into custody, Jesus came into Galilee, preaching the gospel of God, and saying, 'The time is fulfilled, and the kingdom of God is at hand; repent and believe in the gospel'" (Mk. 1:14–15). Now we read that Jesus "went out again by the seashore; and all the multitude were coming to Him, and He was teaching them" (Mk. 2:13). The *again* refers back to what He was doing when He first called others to follow Him. Now he is about to call another.

He calls us too.

---

[5] I took this chart almost verbatim from Austin Farrar's *A Study in Saint Mark* (New York, Oxford Univ. Press, 1952), 66.

Mark 2:14–3:12

Calling, Conflict, & Restoration

Jesus began his ministry trying to avoid conflict by silencing demons and exhorting those whom He cleansed to not spread stories but rather to submit to the administration of Moses. Now that conflict has broken out into the open with the healing of the paralytic, we might expect more conflicts to ensue.

We will not be disappointed.

CALLED—AND HEALED—FOR THE FEAST (2:14–17)

When Jesus called the first four disciples, He entered their house and performed a healing so that they could be served as guests there (Mk. 1:16–20, 29–31). The story of the synagogue exorcism comes in between (1:21–28), but Mark makes a point of reciting the four names again to put us in mind of their calling.

Here the two stages are given to us without any interruption. Jesus calls Levi to leave his job (Mk. 2:14) and then eats with him (v. 15). This meal is not made possible by raising up a hostess from a bed as Jesus had done before, but when the Pharisees challenge Him, His reply uses an analogy to healing which reveals the significance of His healings: "It is not those who are healthy who need a physician, but those who are sick; I did not come to call the righteous, but sinners" (v. 17).

Without doubt, the "sick" are sinners and the "physician" is the one with the authority to forgive sins. Jesus is referring to the claim He has made just before in the synagogue: If He can heal the paralytic, then He must be able to forgive sins. Jesus is able to eat with sinners because He is able to forgive them their sins. And so it is to this day. We eat and drink bread and wine with Jesus at the sacrament of the Lord's Supper for no other reason than that he continues to forgive our sins.

JESUS' DINNER ETIQUETTE

Since we are about to discuss two more conflicts over the way Jesus and His disciples eat, it may be good to point out here how crucial eating and drinking were to the work of Jesus. Jesus' message was in great measure an invitation to a party. It was virtually a dinner club roaming around ancient Palestine. Indeed, when we come to Jesus' last Passover as recorded by Mark and wish to understand what Jesus was doing when He established the Lord's Supper, we must not rip it out of the context of His general dinner etiquette.

Let us take the word of Christ's enemies at face value. Jesus came eating and drinking, and they called him a glutton and a drunkard, a friend of tax gatherers and sinners (Lk. 7:34). Yet they knew that Jesus Himself had not gorged himself nor gone on a bender. He enjoyed His food and His wine, but He enjoyed most of all the company of other people around the dinner table. Jesus spent a great deal of time talking about table manners. His view of how one should eat and drink got Him into many conflicts.

These conflicts vary, as we will see as we continue through Mark. The root problem is the one shown here in Jesus' eating with Levi and his friends. The additional provocation that Jesus gave to the scribes and Pharisees was the company He would keep, especially around the dinner table. Jesus would eat and drink with "many tax-gatherers and others" (Lk. 5:27–38; Mt. 9:9–13; Lk. 7:36–50; Lk. 15:1–2). This was a horrible offense in the eyes of various religious and political leaders.

Would anyone accuse you of being a glutton and a drunkard based on the company you keep at the dinner table?

These conflicts continue in the early Church. What was Peter accused of when He baptized Cornelius and his household (Acts 11:3)? "You went to uncircumcised men and ate with them." How does the Apostle Paul introduce his defense of the gospel in his letter to the Galatians?

But when Cephas came to Antioch, I opposed him to his face, because he stood condemned. For prior to the coming of certain men from James, *he used to eat with the Gentiles*; but when they came, he began to withdraw and hold himself aloof, fearing the party of the circumcision. And the rest of the Jews joined him in hypocrisy; with the result that even Barnabas was carried away by their hypocrisy. But when I saw that they *were not straightforward about the truth of the gospel* . . . .(Gal. 2:11–14a; emphasis added)

At the time that Paul is writing, Jesus is no longer walking among men as he was before his death and resurrection, yet his ministry of eating and drinking with people continues on and continues to provoke conflict about who should be on the list of invited guests. Through the Church, Jesus continues to eat and drink with sinners. He does this especially and formally through the sacrament of the Lord's Supper. He also does this generally and informally through the practice of Christian hospitality.

Consider what Paul had to tell the Corinthians:

I wrote you in my letter not to associate with immoral people; I did not at all mean with the immoral people of this world, or with the covetous and swindlers, or with idolaters; for then you would have to go out of the world. But actually, I wrote to you not to associate with any so-called brother if he should be an immoral person, or covetous, or an idolater, or a reviler, or a drunkard, or a swindler—not even to eat with such a one. For what have I to do with judging outsiders? Do you not judge those who are within the church? But those who are outside, God judges. "Remove the wicked man from among yourselves." (1 Cor. 5:11–13)

Notice, here is another instance where "whom" one eats with is of great importance—just as it was in Jesus' day. Notice also that there is an impulse to refuse to eat with outsiders on the grounds that they are participants in all sorts of sinful lifestyles. Yes they are, but that is not supposed to be a bar to table fellowship.

Is this how we normally think? Don't we normally want to welcome to our table those who have no time for the Church despite being baptized into its membership and having once participated in sacramental communion? But we hold ourselves aloof from the "riff-raff" that has never seen the inside of a church. The Apostle Paul's challenge to the Corinthians echoes down the corridors of history to challenge each age to eat and drink as God would have them eat and drink with the guests he would want them to have.

Let me assure you that Jesus was simply doing in his ministry, by eating and drinking with sinners, what he had been doing as the Angel of the Lord since the beginning. Why did Yahweh ("the Lord") rescue the Israelites from Egypt? What did Moses tell Pharaoh? "Thus says the LORD, the God of Israel, 'Let My people go that they may celebrate a feast to Me in the wilderness'" (Exod. 5:1b). God wanted table fellowship with Israel. In fact, God wanted table fellowship with *all* Israel. Eventually, Pharaoh tried to compromise and say that the adults but not children, could go feast with the Lord. Moses' reply is rather straightforward about the truth of the Gospel: "We shall go with our young and our old; with our sons and our daughters, with our flocks and our herds we will go, for we must hold a feast to the LORD" (Gen. 10:9). And once they were out of Egypt, Jesus (for that is who the Lord in the Old Testament is) establishes these feasts for everyone in Israel:

> Then you shall celebrate the Feast of Weeks to the LORD your God with a tribute of a freewill offering of your hand, which you shall give just as the LORD your God blesses you; and you shall rejoice before the LORD your God, *you and your son and your daughter and your male and female servants and the Levite who is in your town, and the stranger and the orphan and the widow who are in your midst,* in the place where the LORD your God chooses to establish His name. (Deut. 16:10–11; emphasis added)

> You shall eat in the presence of the LORD your God, at the place where He chooses to establish His name, the tithe of your grain, your new wine, your oil, and the first-born of your herd and your flock, in order that you may learn to fear the LORD your God always. And if the distance is so great for you that you are not able to bring the tithe, since the place where the LORD your God chooses to set His name is too far away from you when the LORD your God blesses you, then you shall exchange it for money, and bind the money in your hand and go to the place which the LORD your God chooses. And you may spend the money for whatever your heart desires, for oxen, or sheep, or wine, or strong drink, or whatever your heart desires; and there you shall eat in the presence of the LORD your God and rejoice, you and your household. Also you shall not neglect the Levite who is in your town, for he has no portion or inheritance among you. (Deut. 14:23–27)

When Jesus is acting like what the Elders of Israel call a glutton and a drunkard, He is actually copying God's behavior as he reads about it in the Old Testament. Actually, Jesus is God; so he is *continuing* God's behavior as recorded in the Old Testament. And in Acts and Galatians and 1 Corinthians, we see the Church attempting to imitate God and continue the ministry of Jesus. From those data points we should be able to extrapolate rather clearly how we are to continue not only fellowshipping at God's Table in the Lord's Supper, but also imitating Jesus in showing and accepting hospitality—in inviting others to dine with us and dining with them—as we show that we are members of Christ in our own homes and in the homes of others.

How can we respond? First of all, by accepting the Lord's gracious invitation and attending His banqueting table. Regular participation in the Lord's Supper continues God's feasts with His people, as those we read about in Deuteronomy, and Jesus' dinners with sinners, such as those we read about in the Gospel of Mark.

But how else should we respond to God's dinner invitation? Very simple: Go thou and do likewise. You get to sit around the Lord's Table. Who gets to sit around your dinner table? God has invited you to eat and drink with Him. Whom do you invite to eat and drink with you at your table? How do you worship a so-called glutton and a drunkard—a friend of tax-gatherers and sinners? The answer should be obvious: you invite your local IRS agents and other such people to your home and wine and dine them.

Maybe you don't know any IRS agents or anyone else who really fits the bill. Well, start small. Start with your neighbors.

NEW FEAST VERSUS OLD FAST (2:18–22)

The questions raised regarding Jesus' eating habits represented a clash between good and evil. Here the debate is simply that of before and after. Not only the Pharisees, but also John's disciples are involved. The issue is not ungodly traditions and separations but rather whether or not the present age should involve regular fasting.

In the first debate, Jesus claimed that He was the physician and therefore could and even should fraternize with the sick. He can forgive sins, therefore He can eat with sinners. In this second debate, Jesus again claims a special title for Himself. He is the bridegroom, and the only rational response is a wedding feast.

But Jesus goes further than merely announcing that it is time to party. He also points out that the party is disruptive. New cloth cannot patch an old garment and old wineskins cannot contain new wine. Jesus may be a prophet (and more than a prophet) of the God of Israel, but His message of the kingdom is such that Israel cannot remain the same institution it once was. Mark does not give us Jesus' pessimistic prediction, but the information he does give makes it impossible not to figure it out for ourselves: "And no one, after drinking old wine wishes for new; for he says, 'The old is good enough'" (Lk. 5:39).

PROGRESSING INTO PARABLES

Referring to Luke's account of this incident gives us some more confirmation of what we might see developing as Jesus goes from controversy to controversy. Mark will not explicitly mention parables until chapter 4, but here we notice that Jesus has already begun to use them. Luke explicitly calls Jesus' answer a parable (5:36).

His first open controversy with the scribes and Pharisees was straightforward and unambiguous: Jesus declared Himself to be the Son of Man who could forgive sins. But when Jesus is confronted at Levi's house, He no longer explicitly mentions forgiveness but takes to Himself the analogous (though accurate as to His miracles) title of "physician." Now He explains Himself in terms of patches and new wine on old garments and in old wineskins. Controversy elicits parables. By the time we reach the events of chapter 4, the controversy will have risen to such a point that Mark will feel it necessary to talk about these parables that Jesus will then be telling in elaborate detail.

DAVID & DOEG (2:23–28)

Our third and final controversy over Jesus' eating habits takes place in a field sown with grain. His disciples picked and ate as they traveled, as the Law of Moses plainly allowed:

> When you enter your neighbor's vineyard, then you may eat grapes until you are fully satisfied, but you shall not put any in your basket. When you enter your neighbor's standing grain, then you may pluck the heads with your hand, but you shall not wield a sickle in your neighbor's standing grain. (Deut. 23:24–25)

The principle here was that God owned all the land of Israel and that He wanted His people, even poor travelers, to be able to eat. Thus, He provided those with land to allow passers-by to pick some fruit to eat.

Did God mean for travelers and poor persons to be restricted from such activity on the Sabbath? Plainly not. For a restriction of that privilege would have meant the hungriest people in society would be forced to endure more hunger. God's Sabbath was meant to liberate such people, not load them down with burdens. To take just one example of Sabbath legislation:

> Like a man hired year by year he shall be with him; he shall not rule over him with severity in your sight. Even if he is not redeemed by these means, he shall still go out in the year of jubilee, he and his sons with him. For the sons of Israel are My servants; they are My servants whom I brought out from the land of Egypt. I am the LORD your God. (Lev. 25:53–55)

One must bear in mind that the year of Jubilee was a Sabbath of Sabbaths. Each seventh year was a Sabbath, and the Jubilee year was the capstone year after the seventh seven-year period. God plainly wants freedom for the captives. He makes it clear that all Israelites, even the poorest, are His servants and need to be treated with the dignity and charity that God has shown them Himself. Those whom He has redeemed from Egypt must not be allowed to languish in bondage. The Sabbath was made for such people.

FOR THE SABBATH WAS MADE FOR MAN

The Pharisees had decided that this lawful activity was not permitted on the Sabbath—that those without food storage systems would just have to tighten their belts that day. How could they think that this was a God-honoring application of the Sabbath? Perhaps they cited manna as a precedent—which was not to be gathered on the Sabbath (Exod. 16:22–30). But manna was permitted to be gathered and stored before the Sabbath, which is exactly what Deuteronomy 23 forbids. Furthermore, the Israelites were also prohibited from cooking manna, yet cooking in other cases is allowed on the Sabbath. As Nehemiah writes:

> Moreover, there were at my table one hundred and fifty Jews and officials, besides those who came to us from the nations that were around us. Now that which was prepared for each day was one ox and six choice sheep, also birds were prepared for me; and once in ten days all sorts of wine were furnished in abundance. Yet for all this I did not demand the governor's food allowance, because the servitude was heavy on this people. Remember me, O my God, for good, according to all that I have done for this people. (Neh. 5:17–19)

Nehemiah is hardly susceptible to the charge of laxness regarding the Sabbath, yet he had his servants preparing food every day. If one is permitted to cook on the Sabbath despite the restriction regarding cooking the manna in the wilderness, then how can one claim that the restriction on gathering manna applies to all other gathering of food?

None of this prevented the Pharisees from declaring what Jesus' disciples did to be illegal. They were wrong and the oddity of this passage is that Jesus does not tell them so. Jesus could have told them that their customs were corrupt, just as He later does when confronted about His disciples not ceremonially cleansing their hands before eating (Mk. 7:1ff). Instead, He takes the opportunity to yet again point to His own unique authority. First he was the Son of Man, and then the Physician, and then the Bridegroom, and now He is the Son of Man again and David leading his warriors through the countryside to escape from Saul.

DAVID HUNGERING

Jesus appeals to the precedent of David, the anointed one who was given holy bread for himself and his men. If we interpret this as a justified instance of setting aside a law, then we will misconstrue what Jesus is saying and what happened when Ahimelech gave David bread. The event is recorded in 1 Samuel 21 and needs to be refreshed in our memories if we are to understand Jesus' point.

Then David came to Nob to Ahimelech the priest; and Ahimelech came trembling to meet David, and said to him, "Why are you alone and no one with you?" And David said to Ahimelech the priest, "The king has commissioned me with a matter, and has said to me, 'Let no one know anything about the matter on which I am sending you and with which I have commissioned you; and I have directed the young men to a certain place.' Now therefore, what is under your hand? Give in my hand five loaves of bread, or whatever can be found." And the priest answered David and said, "There is no ordinary bread on hand, but there is consecrated bread; if only the young men have kept themselves from women." And David answered the priest and said to him, "Surely women have been kept from us as previously when I set out and the vessels of the young men were holy, though it was an ordinary journey; how much more then today will their vessels be holy?" So the priest gave him consecrated bread; for there was no bread there but the bread of the Presence which was removed from before the LORD, in order to put hot bread in its place when it was taken away. Now one of the servants of Saul was there that day, detained before the LORD; and his name was Doeg the Edomite, the chief of Saul's shepherds.

Now there are several interesting things about this passage and Jesus' use of it, but first and foremost notice that Ahimelech and David both seem blissfully unaware they are doing anything wrong. Ahimelech wants to be sure that David and his men are ceremonially clean. Sex with women is not somehow unholy. But according to the Mosaic holiness code, being in contact with fluids from within the flesh always makes a person unclean. If Ahimelech was willing to violate God's law by giving the Bread of the Presence to laymen, why is he so concerned to make sure that God's law is not being violated regarding unclean people coming into contact with holy food? This is odd behaviour for one about to commit a lawless act.

Jesus himself characterizes David's action as "not lawful," but what if Jesus is using the Pharisees own thinking and trying to refute it? Notice the parallel account in Matthew 12 which records Jesus' statement: "Or have you not read in the Law, that on the Sabbath the priests in the temple break the Sabbath, and are innocent?" This is an absurd claim articulated to demonstrate the absurdity of the Pharisees. Surely, we know that the priest carrying out their duties given to them to do on the Sabbath are not guilty of breaking the Sabbath! On the contrary, they would be breaking the Sabbath to refrain from those duties.

David's activity with the showbread, then, was "not lawful" in the same sense that the priests "break the Sabbath." David was at war. According to his story he was on a special secret commission for Saul. According to the truth, he was God's anointed fleeing to escape a corrupt king and plant the seeds of his new kingdom. Ahimelech had every reason to believe that David was authorized, under those circumstances, to eat holy bread. If we listen to the Law we will see soldiers at camp and priests in the sanctuary had similar privileges and responsibilities:

> When you go out as an army against your enemies, then you shall keep yourself from every evil thing. If there is among you any man who is unclean because of a nocturnal emission, then he must go outside the camp; he may not reenter the camp. But it shall be when evening approaches, he shall bathe himself with water, and at sundown he may reenter the camp. You shall also have a place outside the camp and go out there, and you shall have a spade among your tools, and it shall be when you sit down outside, you shall dig with it and shall turn to cover up your excrement. Since the LORD your God walks in the midst of your camp to deliver you and to defeat your enemies before you, therefore your camp must be holy; and He must not see anything indecent among you lest He turn away from you. (Deut. 23:9–14)

Like priests serving at the Temple, soldiers in the camp must maintain a heightened level of cleanliness. This is precisely what Ahimelech wanted to make sure that David and his men had been doing. The foundational exhortation to keep from women is found in Exodus 19:15, where Moses tells the Israelites to prepare for God's looming descent and landing onto Mount Sinai. According to Deuteronomy 23, God is similarly present in the war camp. Thus the soldiers needed to keep out of God's sight the things which come from within their flesh. While on a mission, their status was raised by God's presence among them just as he was normally only present among the priests of the sanctuary. In a sense, they became temporary priests.

So Jesus is not claiming by David's example that the Sabbath law can be set aside for the good of humanity, even though He would no doubt say (and is recorded as saying in Mt. 12:7) that applications of the Sabbath principle must be ones that follow through on the Sabbatarian concern for those who are oppressed and afflicted. Rather, He is claiming that His work, as one analogous to David, is a proper Sabbath work for Himself in His office and those whom He has appointed as His servants. Like a holy warrior being permitted holy bread or like a priest offering the morning sacrifice on the Sabbath, Jesus is authorized to feed His men.

Indeed, He is authorized to feed the world. David asked for five loaves to feed himself and his companions. Mark will show us later what David's greater son can do with five loaves to feed five thousand men.

THE SON OF MAN AGAIN

This is the second time that Jesus has dropped the title "Son of Man." Why? Perhaps in this case the answer should be sought in the original week of creation. If one looks at the seven days, one might decide that the creatures of the lesser days are created for the sake of the greater days. Man is created on the sixth day after the animals have been made. The Sabbath is established on the seventh day. Thus, one might reason, man was made for the Sabbath just as the vegetation of Day Three or the fish of Day Five were made for man. Jesus is denying this line of reasoning.[1]

However, a better rationale can probably be found if we think about the nature of the Sabbath and how it relates to the enthronement of the Son of Man in Daniel 7. For the Sabbath was the day of God's enthronement when He rested from the establishment of His dominion with His army arrayed before Him:

> Then the heavens and the earth were completed, and all their armies. And by the seventh day God completed His work which He had done; and He rested on the seventh day from all His work which He had done. Then God blessed the seventh day and sanctified it, because in it He rested from all His work which God had created and made. (Gen. 2:1–2)

Compare this to David, for whom rest signified the completion

---

[1] Austin Farrer, *A Study in Saint Mark* (New York: Oxford Univ. Press, 1952), 275.

of the work of gaining victory over his enemies and thus entailed the establishment of his own throne.

> Now it came about when the king lived in his house, and the LORD had given him rest on every side from all his enemies, that the king said to Nathan the prophet, "See now, I dwell in a house of cedar, but the ark of God dwells within tent curtains." (2 Sam. 7:1–2)

Here we see David "given rest"—and thus enthroned in his palace—considering how God should be enthroned in one of His own. Indeed, the reason God does not permit such a new royal dwelling for Himself to be built is that David's rest is not complete and thus his throne not established as firmly as it should be.

> And David said to Solomon, "My son, I had intended to build a house to the name of the LORD my God. But the word of the LORD came to me, saying, 'You have shed much blood, and have waged great wars; you shall not build a house to My name, because you have shed so much blood on the earth before Me. Behold, a son shall be born to you, who shall be *a man of rest*; and I will *give him rest from all his enemies on every side*; for his name shall be Solomon, and I will give peace and quiet to Israel in his days. He shall build a house for My name, and he shall be My son, and I will be his father; and I will *establish the throne* of his kingdom over Israel forever.'" (1 Chr. 22:7–10; emphasis added)

Thus, if Jesus is the Son of Man, then He is destined to be enthroned with God as Daniel saw in his vision. The enthronement of the Son of Adam reveals that the Sabbath is, by God's grace, the establishment of Man's rest as well as God's. And Jesus, as the Son of Adam has therefore the authority to decide what ought to count as work on the Sabbath and what ought not to count. In this Jesus agreed that such rules had to be laid down by men just as the Pharisees had laid them down. The Pharisaical rules, however, were oppressive, and Jesus claimed for himself the authority to dictate better ones.

Ahimelech gave bread to David on the basis of David's false claim to be under Saul's orders serving in a special secret mission. If he had the status to eat from the Lord's Table, it was because he had been anointed as God's king; and even though that anointing was secret and Saul was yet on the throne, David still had the authority to declare his band of men a legitimate camp of Israel's army. Likewise, Jesus had not yet been enthroned, but only anointed to take the throne. Nevertheless, like David the fugitive who was not yet enthroned, Jesus had the authority to allow His disciples to pick grain and eat it on the Sabbath in contradiction to the Pharisees and their traditions.

The comparison with David points to the irony of Jesus' enthronement in Mark's gospel. When David finally sat on his throne, he was recognized for who he was. But for Jesus, only a pagan centurion would recognize the greater David's enthronement.

SAUL & DOEG

If Jesus claims to be analogous to David, then He is implying the Pharisees are fulfilling the place of Saul. But we need not stop there. There was someone who happened to see David receive the bread from the high priest and then went to Saul and reported it in order to get Ahimelech in trouble. "Now one of the servants of Saul was there that day, detained before the LORD; and his name was Doeg the Edomite, the chief of Saul's shepherds" (1 Sam. 21:7) Unlike John, Mark does not record Jesus railing against false shepherds, but he shows here a comparison between the Pharisees and an Edomite shepherd who betrays David.

ABIATHAR

Thus far, we have treated Jesus' answer to the Pharisees as a straightforward appeal to historical precedent. Such a reply seems rather odd since this is the third of three controversies over food, and in the first two Jesus resorted to parables. But appearances can be misleading. Jesus is here giving the Pharisees a "dark saying of old," a parable (Ps. 78:2). In plain contradiction to the facts of history, Jesus tells the Pharisees that it was Abiathar, not Ahimelech, who was high priest when David took the bread of the Presence.

Instead of treating this as a scribal error, why not assume that Jesus knows exactly what He is saying? Ahimelech was a martyr because he aided the anointed one and was killed by Doeg at Saul's order for doing so. Jesus gets no comparable allegiance from any of the priests of His day, let alone from the high priest. On the other hand, Jesus does things that point to a radical change in the Aaronic priesthood itself. He cleanses a leper and forgives sins and institutes His own feasts with sinners. Temple and Priesthood are forever altered because of David's greater Son.

This explains Jesus' substitution of Abiathar for Ahimelech. David had a greater Son who, in his own lesser but significant way, altered the priesthood and the sanctuary. Solomon built a Temple and reconsolidated Israel's worship. He also changed the priesthood by removing Abiathar, Ahimelech's son, from his office of high priest. Abiathar had at one time served David, but later he supported Solomon's rival for the throne. Solomon's response is recorded in 1 Kings 2:25–26.

> Then to Abiathar the priest the king said, "Go to Anathoth to your own field, for you deserve to die; but I will not put you to death at this time, because you carried the ark of the Lord GOD before my father David, and because you were afflicted in everything with which my father was afflicted." So Solomon dismissed Abiathar from being priest to the LORD, in order to fulfill the word of the LORD, which He had spoken concerning the house of Eli in Shiloh.

A cryptic reference to the wrong priest in Jesus' reply to the Pharisees is not without meaning. Jesus is hinting at what He will plainly say: that the Temple and Priesthood are going to be dispensed with in their present form; that they have been disloyal to God and are under judgment.

From what we know of the Pharisees, they themselves would have been happy to see the Priesthood judged and replaced. The priests were mostly Sadducees, disbelievers in the resurrection and kept in power because they served Roman interests. Nevertheless, Jesus viewed both groups as parts and perpetuators of one corrupt system and taught that judgment of one would include the judgment of the other. As Solomon decided in the case of Abiathar, he would give their office to another.

The Son of Man has authority on earth to bring greater judgments than either David or Solomon.

KILLING THE SABBATH (3:1–6)

Jesus, we are told, came into a synagogue "again," reminding us of His previous such visit where, as if He were in the wilderness, He encountered a servant of Satan. It is still the Sabbath, the same day as the incident regarding the disciples' picking of grain. Mark tells us that "they" were spying on Jesus, referring back to the same Pharisees who had accused the disciples of breaking the Sabbath. The fact that the Pharisees end up going to the Herodians also continues the theme begun in the last paragraph: Herod was an Edomite. The Pharisees are taking sides with Doeg.

In Jesus' first controversy in which He claimed to be the Son of Man and to have the authority to forgive sins, Jesus proved His claim by healing the paralytic. Here we see the same thing happening, though told in two successive paragraphs. Jesus has claimed to be the Son of Man and to have authority to decide what is lawful on the Sabbath. Now He proves His claim by healing the man with the withered hand.

Reflecting on the blessings and curses which Moses placed before Israel as a choice between life and death (Deut. 30:15ff), Solomon presented wisdom as a way of life and foolishness as a way of death.

> He who is steadfast in righteousness will attain to life,
> And he who pursues evil will bring about his own death.
> (Prov. 11:19)
>
> In the way of righteousness is life,
> And in its pathway there is no death. (Prov. 12:28)
>
> The teaching of the wise is a fountain of life,
> To turn aside from the snares of death. (Prov. 13:14)
>
> The fear of the LORD is a fountain of life,
> That one may avoid the snares of death. (Prov. 14:27)

Jesus thus presents the Pharisees with rather polarized alternatives reflecting the Law of Moses and the wisdom of Solomon. Do the Pharisees wish to help or to harm, to save a life or to kill? One would expect them to reply that there are other alternatives such as waiting until the next day to heal the hand (cf. Lk. 13:14). But they keep silent.

Or do they? Jesus is not the sort of interrogator one can avoid answering. Actions speak louder than words. The Pharisees "immediately" go to the Herodians to make a plan that very same day. Their answer is clear: "In your case, Jesus, it is lawful to harm and to kill on the Sabbath."

THE SIGN OF THE RESTORED HAND

Jesus commands the man whom He has raised up to stretch out his hand (Mk. 3:5). Adam and Eve were thrown out of the garden because one of them "might stretch out his hand, and take also from the tree of life, and eat, and live forever." Giving back to a man his grasp hints that the tree of life in the sanctuary might again be given back to man.

Moses also was given a sign of a diseased hand—in his case a leprous one which God miraculously sickened and then healed (Exod. 4:6–7). Just as the Lord's anger burned against Moses when, despite the signs, he still didn't trust in God's power (vv. 10–14), the anger of Jesus burned against the religious leaders of Israel (Mk. 3:5).

But the unbelief of the Pharisees is far more serious than Moses' temporary doubts. Moses performed the sign of the restored hand before "the elders of Israel" and they believed (Exod. 4:29–31). Pharaoh's heart was hardened, however, despite experiencing much greater and much more afflicting signs. For Jesus it is the elders of Israel, the religious leaders, whose hearts are hardened (Mk. 3:5).

The Pharisees' silence in response to the probing questions of Jesus in the presence of a useless hand also points to a Psalm from the time of the exile. The writer calls down a malediction on his own head, singing:

> If I forget you, O Jerusalem,
> May my right hand forget her skill.
> May my tongue cleave to the roof of my mouth,
> If I do not remember you,
> If I do not exalt Jerusalem
> Above my chief joy. (Ps. 137:5–6)

The Pharisees no doubt thought they had to oppose Jesus precisely because He was not exalting Jerusalem. But Jesus claimed that He was greater than Jerusalem, and that would mean that the Pharisees are the ones violating the spirit of this passage. Or to put it another way, Jesus is the true Jerusalem of which the city of David in Palestine is but a shadow. By attacking Jesus, the Pharisees are attacking Jerusalem. Indeed, they go to the loyalists of an Edomite ruler to carry out their attack. The very next verse of Psalm 137 reads:

> Remember, O Lord, against the sons of Edom
> The day of Jerusalem,
> Who said, "Raze it, raze it
> To its very foundation."

Since we have seen that Mark has a special concern to show how Jesus was prophesied by the Kingdom era in Israel's history, perhaps we should turn to that period. A withered hand in a synagogue may not be the personal fault of anyone, but Psalm 32 indicates that it is not a good sign. As David sang:

> When I kept silent [about my sin], my body wasted away
> Through my groaning all day long.
> For day and night Your hand was heavy upon me;
> My life juices were turned into the drought of summer .(vv. 3–4)

Thus, it is quite possible to see the deformity of the withered hand as a scandal in the synagogue. Whatever may be the case, the hand's restoration would certainly hold out the promise of the forgiveness of sins.

JEROBOAM & THE PHARISEES

The most direct precedent for the restoration of the withered hand, however, is the only other restoration of a withered hand in the Scriptures. In 1 Kings 13 we read how King Jeroboam was confronted by "the man of God" for building idol shrines for the tribes of the Northern Kingdom. When the man of God met him at his false altar and warned him of divine wrath, the king "stretched out his hand from the altar, saying, 'Seize him.' But his hand which he stretched out against him dried up, so that he could not draw it back to himself" (v. 4).

Jeroboam was wise enough to know when to stop warring against God's prophet. He immediately begged the man of God to pray for him so that he would be healed. The prophet was willing to pray and God answered the prayer by healing Jeroboam's withered hand.

The common object in the two stories is the healing of a withered hand. But note the significant contrast between how the idolater Jeroboam responded to the withered hand and how the Pharisees responded to it. Jeroboam wanted to be healed; the Pharisees wanted to kill Jesus for daring to heal. The one who established worship at unauthorized shrines had better discernment than those who prided themselves for their alleged devotion to God.

Indeed, there is another aspect to this contrast between Jeroboam and the Pharisees. Once Jeroboam is healed, he responds with a concrete expression of gratitude and reconciliation.

> Then the king said to the man of God, "Come home with me and refresh yourself, and I will give you a reward." But the man of God said to the king, "If you were to give me half your house I would not go with you, nor would I eat bread or drink water in this place. "For so it was commanded me by the word of the LORD, saying, 'You shall eat no bread, nor drink water, nor return by the way which you came.'" (1 Kgs. 7–9)

Jeroboam was thankful for being healed and therefore invited the prophet to eat with him. His invitation was turned down, however, because the man of God was fasting by God's command. Jesus is known to be under no obligation to fast. He invites all to eat with Him, even those hungry on the road during a Sabbath day. Yet instead of following Jeroboam's correct example and inviting Jesus to eat and drink with them, the Pharisees criticize Him for eating and drinking too much.

Unlike the prophets of old, Jesus does not have to rebuke the Jews for worshiping at idol-shrines where they claimed that golden calves could be used as mediators between God and man. Israel had, by God's grace, reached the point where they firmly resisted idolatry. And yet, for all that, they had reached a low point in their history. They were worse than idolaters. In fact, the parallelism between the two stories leaves us wondering if Mark does not want us to think of the synagogue as something on the order of Jeroboam's wicked altar.

RESTORATION FROM IDOLATRY

The very nature of Jesus' healing miracles point to Israel's idolatry. Jesus seems to perform three types of miracles: exorcisms, cleansings, and restorations. The exorcisms and cleansings belong together because, in Mark's language, Jesus casts out "unclean" spirits. His restorations, however, involve other sorts of infirmities or diseases, though they are sometimes linked to exorcisms when a demon is said to cause a specific illness.

There have been three such restorations thus far: a woman raised up who was prone with a fever, a paralytic on a mat healed, and a man's withered hand restored. Later we will read about a girl raised from the dead, a deaf-mute healed, a blind man cured, another deaf-mute healed, and yet another blind man healed.

With two exceptions, we find complementary healings following on one another. The paralytic must be restored to walking. His feet and legs are thus made central to his restoration. The withered hand rather nicely complements the useless feet of the paralytic. So also, we find ears and mouths being opened and then eyes. This pattern is presented to us twice in the same order to make sure we don't miss it.

But what about Simon's mother-in-law and Jairus' daughter, neither of whom is followed by what seems like a complement? In the case of Jairus' daughter, the answer is simple enough: Resurrection can be given no complement; it is complete in itself. In the case of Simon's mother-in-law, it may be that Mark interpreted a fever as a whole-body ailment which had no ready complement.[2]

What we have here is a rather intentional portrayal of the complete restoration of humanity. Restoration from what? Hear the Word of the Lord:

---

[2] There is another—and I believe—better explanation for why Mark recounts no miraculous restoration to complement the raising of Simon's mother-in-law. Austin Farrer, in his *A Study in Saint Mark*, identifies four major cycles of miracles (page 42):

1. Exorcism; Restoration; Cleansing; Restoration—Complement Restoration
2. Exorcisms; Re[Cleansing]storation
3. Exorcism; Restoration—Complement Restoration
4. Exorcisive Restoration—Complement Restoration

> For the LORD will judge His people,
> And will have compassion on His servants.
> The idols of the nations are but silver and gold,
> The work of man's hands.
> They have mouths, but they do not speak;
> They have eyes, but they do not see;
> They have ears, but they do not hear;
> Nor is there any breath at all in their mouths.
> Those who make them will be like them,
> Yes, everyone who trusts in them. (Ps. 135:14–18; cf., 115:4–8)

Idolatry can be present even where there are no acknowledged idols of silver and gold. Jesus' miracles point to the practice of a more subtle—and thus more deadly—idolatry than that which took place at the time of Jeroboam. The miracles are a sign that the Jews have been conformed to the pattern of man–made images. Jesus, as the image of God, must restore them to the God–made pattern. He wants them to be human again.

RETREAT & REGROUP (3:7–12)

The Pharisees believe they're human enough; their murderous plotting drives Jesus away. The text says that Jesus "withdrew" (NASB). In context, it would be better to say that Jesus fled. Matthew uses the same word to describe Joseph taking his family and fleeing from Herod (Mt. 2:14), and the Greek translation of the Hebrew Scriptures uses it to describe David fleeing from Saul's mis-aimed spear (1 Sam. 19:10). Indeed it is used in that translation to describe a fleeing army (Josh. 8:15). Jesus was escaping danger.

As we will see, the integrity of each of these cycles is further established by the fact that each one contains a parent or child being healed at the intercession of the person's parent or child. Aside from the complements, Mark gives us a straightforward 4, 3, 2, 1 pattern. Each major cycle begins with an exorcism followed by a restoration. In the case of second major cycle, Mark uses the sandwiched stories of the raising of Jairus' daughter and the woman with the issue of blood so that he ends the cycle with a restoration *and* has a restoration follow after the exorcism.

The complementary miracles are actually their own miniature cycles. Jesus calls the first four disciples and then calls another disciple following the same pattern used to call each of the first.

Yet others flock to him. When David fled from Saul after getting the bread from Ahimelech, he fled to the cave of Adullam. "And everyone who was in distress, and everyone who was in debt, and everyone who was discontented, gathered to him; and he became captain over them" (1 Sam. 22:2). But David only collected four hundred. Jesus seems to have attracted a vast multitude not only from Israel proper but also from Gentile lands.

David regrouped in a cave, but Jesus in a boat. Considering where He was when He called Peter and his friends and then when He called Levi, it seems that Jesus might issue another call.

The First Resurrection

The Pharisees have definitively rejected Jesus, as is proven by their conspiring with loyalists of their enemy Herod in order to kill him. Yet He seems to draw almost everyone else to Himself. Does this mean that Jesus will become an acknowledged king like David once did? Mark's last paragraph gave us hope that most of the people of Israel would recognize Him.

In this next section, we get our first strong hint that Jesus' quarrel is not only with the Pharisees but with others as well. Not only is Judas' pending betrayal mentioned early on—the first mention of Jesus' death in Mark's gospel—but the section then details the unbelief of Jesus' own family. The incident, so near the beginning of this section, of the family disbelieving makes a nice bookend for the last paragraph of the section, which records Jesus being rejected by His hometown. The Pharisees are not the only Israelites with hardened hearts.

CALLING THE TWELVE (3:13–19)

David became a captain to the men he gathered to himself. Jesus too is a captain of a great host and decides to train and equip men under Him. The militaristic nature of Jesus' commission is underscored by the fact that preaching is accompanied by the driving out of the demons—demons who will later be compared to strong men who must be bound and to legions of warriors.

More than an army, Jesus acts in such a way as to indicate that His followers are to be a new Israel. Like He did as the Angel of the Lord with Moses on Mount Sinai with the twelve tribes, Jesus now goes up a mountain and selects twelve men to represent a new version of the twelve tribes.

Before this point in his story, Mark has told us about the callings of five men: Simon, Andrew, James, and John from their boats and Levi from his money table. It is interesting to see how those names are listed with the new ones.

In the first place, Simon, James, and John are not only listed first, but also given new names. Andrew who was called with Peter is now separated from him. David had three special men (1 Sam. 8:11–17), and so does Jesus. The difference, however, is that David's three friends risked their lives for their king and offered him a cup to drink at the risk of their own blood. This time it is the greater David who will make the offer to His three men.

CALLING & HEALING

Another surprise is that Levi's name has been changed to Matthew. Indeed, if it weren't for the witness of Matthew's gospel, we wouldn't even know that they were the same person. What we are left with, then, is not seven, but eight new names who have been chosen and called into service. Correspondingly, there are to be eight new healing miracles in Mark's Gospel: the Gerasene demoniac, the woman with the issue of blood, Jairus' daughter, the Syro-Phoenician woman's daughter, the demon-possessed boy at the Mount of Transfiguration, the deaf mute, the blind man, the demon-possessed deaf mute, and blind Bartimaeus.

This correspondence should not surprise us if we have been paying attention to what Mark has already told us. First, he wrote of the seaside calling of four disciples from the midst of their vocation. He then relates four accounts of individual healings. Yes, there are times when Mark tells us of a great many healings, but his stories of individuals always stand out. He never tells us of the healing of two blind men as Matthew does or of the cleansing of twelve lepers at once as Luke does. In the wake of the calling of the four, he gives us the healing of the four: the synagogue demoniac, the mother-in-law of Simon, the leper, and the paralytic. Mark then begins a new cycle with another seaside calling of one from the midst of his vocation. Corresponding to the singular calling, Mark gives us an account of one miracle, the restoration of the withered hand. As we've mentioned, this second shorter cycle is the complement of the first. The withered hand's restoration completes the climax of the first cycle in which the paralytic is restored to walking.

Mark's point is quite simple. Calling and restoration belong together. When God calls us to serve, He must enable us to serve if we are to fulfill His calling. When God calls us to serve, we can be confident that God has restored us and forgiven us so that we can do so.

RESTORATION TO PRIESTHOOD

It might be helpful to think about the Old Testament background that was certainly assumed by all four Gospel writers as they selected which miraculous healings to report to us. Jesus, in Mark's gospel, has already explicitly compared healing to forgiveness and restoration to fellowship (Mk. 2:9–11, 16–17). This analogy involves a correspondence between sickness or deformity and sin. It is an analogy the Israelites would be familiar with, since under the Mosaic covenant such things prevented one from coming into God's presence in the Tabernacle.

> Then the LORD spoke to Moses, saying, "Speak to Aaron, saying, 'No man of your offspring throughout their generations who has a defect shall approach to offer the bread of his God. For no one who has a defect shall approach: a blind man, or a lame man, or he who has a disfigured face, or any deformed limb, or a man who has a broken foot or broken hand, or a hunchback or a dwarf, or one who has a defect in his eye or eczema or scabs or crushed testicles. No man among the descendants of Aaron the priest, who has a defect, is to come near to offer the LORD's offerings by fire; since he has a defect, he shall not come near to offer the bread of his God. He may eat the bread of his God, both of the most holy and of the holy, only he shall not go in to the veil or come near the altar because he has a defect, that he may not profane My sanctuaries. For I am the LORD who sanctifies them ... No man, of the descendants of Aaron, who is a leper or who has a discharge, may eat of the holy gifts until he is clean.'" (Lev. 21:16–23; 22:4)

These requirements are only placed on the Aaronic priesthood, with the exception of the prohibition on lepers and other unclean people eating from the altar. Nevertheless, all Israel is a nation of priests (Exod. 19:5–6). Jesus is restoring Israel to the priesthood, to the service of God's house (which ultimately is Israel herself). His miracles point to that restoration.

THE BETRAYER

With the calling of the Twelve, we get our first direct reference to Jesus' appointment with death. Judas is listed as the one who betrayed him. When Jesus first called Simon and his companion, we were told of the imprisonment of John the Baptist. When Jesus next sends the twelve on a mission, Mark will find it is an appropriate place to mention John's martyrdom. The call to service is a call to sacrifice. Jesus' own baptism was His commission to die, and it is the foundation of His authority to call and to forgive us.

FAMILY & PHARISEES (3:20–35)

After summoning His first four disciples, Jesus came to their home and ate with them, restoring Simon's mother-in-law to health so that she could serve. After summoning Levi to be His disciple, Jesus ate and drank with him and his companions in his home, stating that He did so because He was the "physician" who could restore the "sick." Now He has again come home after issuing a summons, and He again tries to eat. But this time His meal cannot take place. Jesus is too overwhelmed. The mobbing has reached the point where He can barely function.

NEW COVENANT FAMILY

When David fled from Saul, he went to Gath. There, in order to preserve his life from the King, he feigned madness so that the king did not view him as a threat. He was able to flee from there to the cave of Adullam where he collected men around him. His family came to him as well. He took them to a place of refuge out of Saul's reach so that they would be protected (1 Sam. 22:1–3).

With the greater David, the situation is much worse. Though Jesus is trying to avoid conflict by preventing demons from speaking, He is not pretending to be insane. Nevertheless, not a Gentile ruler, but His "own people" (Mk. 3:21) believe that He has lost His mind. Instead of Him providing for them, they come and try to take custody of Him. This leads to Jesus claiming a new family.

In the middle of this scenario, we have the Jerusalem scribes claiming that Jesus is more than crazy; He is demonic. It seems that the more closely one is associated with the central sanctuary—the Temple in Jerusalem—the more depraved one is likely to be. Neither group believes in Jesus, but at least His own kinsmen don't claim He is possessed!

This will not be the only time Mark sandwiches one story within another. What is the relationship between the accusation of the scribes and the unbelief of Jesus' family? If we understand the scribes to be religious leaders in Israel, the nature of God's covenant with Israel is probably in view. That covenant from the time of Abraham was one in which the family was primary. But no longer. Just as Jesus is His own Temple and Priesthood where the forgiveness of sins is granted, so He is the head of a new "family" no longer based on blood but on faith and obedience. "For whoever does the will of God, he is my brother and sister and mother."

THE PARABLE OF THE BOUND STRONG MAN

The scribes accuse Jesus of being in league with a chief demon so that He could cast out other demons. Jesus replies by a parable. A house divided cannot stand. If Satan were at war with Satan, then Satan's kingdom would be no threat and no power. But it is a power. Thus, Satan's house must be unified, and he is not in the practice of casting out demons.

But if his house does stand, then how is Jesus able to break into it? It is not possible unless Jesus has first bound the strong man. Jesus doesn't say that *when* one robs a house one must overcome the strong man in the house. Rather He presents a temporal and causal order: One must *first* bind the strong man and then freely take from his house. Jesus is rescuing people from Satan's household because He has previously defeated Satan himself.

Jesus is pointing back to what took place in the wilderness when He and Satan engaged in combat. The Israelites defeated the Philistines because David slew Goliath. So Satan's underlings are under Jesus' power because Jesus overcame Satan himself. Because Jesus has bound the strong man, none of the weaker demons can do anything to stop Him from rescuing those they have possessed.

There may be more to Jesus' statements about a "house divided" than merely a statement about why Satan could not be casting out demons. Mark speaks of this as a "parable," and, as we will soon see, "parables" are usually told to bring judgment on the hearers. Perhaps Jesus is alluding to another house, the House of Israel that is split among competing factions and will not stand much longer.

BLASPHEMY AGAINST THE HOLY SPIRIT

John prophesied that Jesus would baptize with the Holy Spirit, and at John's baptism the Holy Spirit came upon Jesus. Jesus received His Pentecost at the Jordan so that He would be able to accomplish His mission and arrange a Pentecost in Jerusalem for His followers. Thus, we have two stages set forth for us in Mark's Gospel: the ministry of the Son and then the ministry of the Spirit. Though the Spirit is unquestionably present in Jesus, it has not yet flowed out of Jesus to others, as it will on the day of Pentecost.

The scribes from Jerusalem are rejecting Jesus, and that is a momentous error. But it is not absolutely fatal. What the scribes from Jerusalem reject in Galilee will be offered again in Jerusalem by disciples from Galilee. The Holy Spirit will come upon the disciples and they will witness to the scribes. At that point, everything will still be forgivable. The great day of vengeance will still not fall on the city that has murdered the Son of God if they repent. But if this second witness—the witness of the Spirit—is spoken against, then time will run out and the wrath of God will fall.

What Mark leaves relatively unexplained, Luke clearly spells out by recording Jesus' exhortation to His disciples to bear witness for him when His time comes:

> And I say to you, everyone who confesses Me before men, the Son of Man shall confess him also before the angels of God; but he who denies Me before men shall be denied before the angels of God. And everyone who will speak a word against the Son of Man, it shall be forgiven him; but he who blasphemes against the Holy Spirit, it shall not be forgiven him. And when they bring you before the synagogues and the rulers and the authorities, do not become anxious about how or what you should speak in your defense, or what you should say; for the Holy Spirit will teach you in that very hour what you ought to say. (Lk. 12:9–12)

The blasphemy against the Holy Spirit here is the rejection of the Spirit-taught witnesses who confess the Son of Man before men. Luke not only gives us Jesus' teaching in this regard, but he shows it occurring in the book of Acts: Where Jesus remained silent before the authorities, the disciples boldly declare the gospel.

Mark and Luke are speaking of the same thing. Indeed, in that very quote from Luke, a few sentences earlier, Jesus explicitly tells his disciples that they must eventually broadcast the material He is telling them in secret.

> But there is nothing covered up that will not be revealed, and hidden that will not be known. Accordingly, whatever you have said in the dark shall be heard in the light, and what you have whispered in the inner rooms shall be proclaimed upon the housetops. (Lk. 12:3–4; cf., Mt. 10:26–27)

Mark will record Jesus saying essentially the same thing in just a few paragraphs in the same incident (Mk. 4:21–25).

Blasphemy against the Holy Spirit, then, is not to be explained in terms of some difference in being or eternal status between the Son and the Holy Spirit so that curse words involving Jesus' name are forgivable, but not expletives involving the Spirit. Rather, it refers to the *eschatological framework* of Jesus' work in His own generation. The rejection of Jesus, as serious as that is, does not bring immediate condemnation. Forgiveness is still available. But after rejecting the second witness of the Spirit after Pentecost, time runs out for Israel. There is no forgiveness for blasphemy against the Spirit.

The general application of Jesus' warning against blasphemy against the Holy Spirit is not too hard to figure out:

> A man who hardens his neck after much reproof
> Will suddenly be broken and there is no remedy. (Prov. 29:1)

God sends us different witnesses and warnings via the ministry of the Church both official and unofficial, as well as through providence. He is patient and slow to anger. But if we continue in sin, we will be judged.

The application of Jesus' warning against blasphemy against the Holy Spirit is to repent the first time.

DARK SAYINGS: THE SOILS (4:1–20)

Many things in Mark's Gospel are first recorded almost as if seeds and then appear again in more advanced stages of growth and sometimes decay. When Simon's mother-in-law is raised up to serve, it almost seems strange that one who was sick would be put to work so quickly. (We tend to forget that this was a miraculous recovery that gave her back, in an instant, her health and rest, not a natural recovery that would require time and sleep.) But when we get to the call of Levi, the same pattern is elaborated so that we see that Jesus is restoring and calling people to feast with Him. Yes, Simon's mother-in-law was the hostess, but she was overjoyed to be hosting the Son of David just as Levi was honored to do so. Then after Jesus calls the Twelve, we expect a feast again and are not disappointed. No one eats, but Mark makes a point of telling us that no one is able to eat.

So it is now with the parables. Jesus began speaking in parables from the time He ate with Levi. Mark explicitly called his statements about Satan being divided against Satan, "parables." Now, not only does Jesus use parables, but His disciples also ask about them, and Jesus actually talks about his use of parables. Indeed, as we will see, He tells his parables about parables.

We should also note that by preaching in parables, Jesus is issuing a new sort of calling. He called Simon, Andrew, James, and John by the sea and then Levi and then chose the twelve. Now that those callings have been issued, He is teaching by the seashore, issuing a general call for those with ears to hear.

WHY PARABLES?

The parable of the sower neatly falls into three parts. It begins and ends with the parable itself: first the telling of it to the crowds and then the explaining of it to the disciples. But in between those two sections lies a place where Jesus explains to His disciples why He uses parables (Mk. 4:10–12). Parables are not homely illustrations for agricultural people to find easy to understand. Jesus is perfectly clear that parables are intentionally obscure.

Why would Jesus want to teach in an obscure way that few if

any could understand? One explanation those in the Reformed tradition might find attractive is that Jesus is implementing the doctrine of election. Many are called but few are chosen. That explanation won't work in this case. The doctrine of election states that, apart from those whom the Lord chooses (elects) to change, all people will resist the gospel—not because they don't understand it, but because they don't *like* it. To think that Jesus needed to hide the truth in order to support the doctrine of election is to think too highly of human nature. The problem isn't ultimately in the intellectual grasp of the claims of the Gospel, but rather in how one reacts to those claims. The fact is, Jesus will eventually tell a parable immediately obvious to His listeners, and the result is not His listeners' accepting the truth, but rather their killing Him. The parable of the vineyard will lead directly to His crucifixion precisely because He told it in such a way that the meaning of the parable was unmistakable (Mk. 12:1–12).

But thinking about the parable of the vineyard can give us a clue as to why the parables preceding it are rather unclear. Jesus, remember, first began telling parables in response to opposition. He was willing to clearly confront the Pharisees and scribes with His authority to forgive sins, but once they decided to become hostile rather than overjoyed at the superabundant grace of God, Jesus began giving them allegories about physicians and sick people or dark hints about a priest removed from office. The healing of the paralytic showed Him that plain teaching resulted in plain opposition. He had always known this was likely and had been muzzling the demons to not tell who He was. But Jesus is not in a position to simply cease preaching the good news of the Kingdom. He cannot muzzle himself. So he becomes obscure enough that only those with ears to hear will understand. Those who pay attention to what He is saying and who are willing to think about it and wrestle with it will be rewarded. But those who are not that interested will be passed by, and Jesus' accusers will not have as easy a time finding a basis for making an accusation against Him.

The evidence from the Old Testament indicates that parables are reserved for times of judgment.[1] The singer of Psalm 78 says that

---

[1] Thanks to Jeff Meyers for pointing this out to me.

he will speak a parable or dark saying (Ps. 78:2) and then he goes on to speak of Israel's sins and the judgments that fell on her because of them. Nathan tells David a parable because of David's sin and God's looming judgment on him (2 Sam. 12:1). Gideon's son Jotham told a parable to the men of Shechem because they had chosen the mass-murderer Abimelech to be their king, and he was prophesying that they would come under judgment for killing all of his brothers (Judg. 9:1–21). Ezekiel tells parables of judgment against Israel (Ezek. 17, 24). Corresponding to this, Jesus tells his disciples that He is speaking in parables because Israel is again in a time of judgment. He appeals to the prophecy of Isaiah and the impending judgment in his time to explain the situation:

> And He said, "Go, and tell this people:
> 'Keep on listening, but do not perceive;
> Keep on looking, but do not understand.'
> Render the hearts of this people insensitive,
> Their ears dull,
> And their eyes dim,
> Lest they see with their eyes,
> Hear with their ears,
> Understand with their hearts,
> And return and be healed."
> Then I said, "Lord, how long?"
> And He answered, "Until cities are devastated and without inhabitant,
> Houses are without people,
> And the land is utterly desolate,
> The LORD has removed men far away,
> And the forsaken places are many in the midst of the land." (Is. 6:9–12)

God was prophesying to Isaiah the exile of Judah to Babylon. Military invasion and forced deportation would be God's judgment on Judah for her sins, according to Isaiah. Jesus is claiming Isaiah for His own time. Though Isaiah was speaking of events future to him, but long past to the disciples, Jesus is telling them that those events already past themselves point to a more basic and final judgment on Israel.

We often affirm to others and ourselves that Jesus was more than a mere prophet. But let's not forget that He was never *less* than a prophet. Jesus had a message for His generation: repent or perish. This was not only a message for individuals to make sure they inherited eternal life after they died. It was a message for the entire culture that a great many of them and their children were doomed unless they repented. Isaiah prophesied that the Chaldeans would destroy Jerusalem. In Jesus' day the obvious heirs of the Chaldeans were the Romans. A day was coming when Israel would be destroyed, and Jesus understood Himself to be gathering a remnant to escape that judgment and form a new Israel. Along with Jesus' own impending destruction at the hands of the Romans, the impending destruction of the Temple and Jerusalem are a constant reference point and rationale for Jesus' mission.

THE SEEDS

Jesus' quotation from Isaiah may explain more than simply the looming judgment hanging over Israel. The parable of the soils is also a parable about seed, and Jesus' appeal to Isaiah's commissioning includes a reference to seed in the very next verse:

> "Yet there will be a tenth portion in it,
> And it will again be subject to burning,
> Like a terebinth or an oak
> Whose stump remains when it is felled.
> The holy seed is its stump." (Is. 6:13)

But what happened to that seed? Now, centuries after the return from exile, Jesus is confronted by a seed that seems anything but "holy." Why is this? Commonly this parable is interpreted as a picture of the response to Jesus' own ministry. This *may* be all that Jesus meant by it, but that is not likely. In the context of His reference to Isaiah 6, it would make a great deal of sense for Jesus to be explaining how Israel has fallen away from what God planted them to be when He brought them back from the exile at the time of Ezra, Nehemiah, and Esther. As we will see when we get to Mark 11:15 and Jesus' reference to Isaiah 56:7, Jesus quite firmly believed that His own generation had backslidden away from and fallen short of what they were supposed to be when they returned from exile. More than one prophet explained that return from exile as God's *sowing* or *planting* of them in the Promised Land:

"Behold, days are coming," declares the LORD, "when I will sow the house of Israel and the house of Judah with the seed of man and with the seed of beast. And it will come about that as I have watched over them to pluck up, to break down, to overthrow, to destroy, and to bring disaster, so I will watch over them to build and to plant," declares the LORD. (Jer. 31:27–28)

Then the word of the LORD came to me, saying, "Thus says the LORD God of Israel, 'Like these good figs, so I will regard as good the captives of Judah, whom I have sent out of this place into the land of the Chaldeans. For I will set My eyes on them for good, and I will bring them again to this land; and I will build them up and not overthrow them, and I will plant them and not pluck them up. And I will give them a heart to know Me, for I am the LORD; and they will be My people, and I will be their God, for they will return to Me with their whole heart.'" (Jer. 24:4–7)

"And it will come about in that day that I will respond," declares the LORD. "I will respond to the heavens, and they will respond to the earth, And the earth will respond to the grain, to the new wine, and to the oil, And they will respond to Jezreel.
And I will sow her for Myself in the land.
I will also have compassion on her who had not obtained compassion, And I will say to those who were not My people, 'You are My people!' And they will say, 'You are my God!'" (Hos. 2:21–23)

I will rejoice greatly in the LORD,
My soul will exult in my God;
For He has clothed me with garments of salvation,
He has wrapped me with a robe of righteousness,
As a bridegroom decks himself with a garland,
And as a bride adorns herself with her jewels.
For as the earth brings forth its sprouts,
And as a garden causes the things sown in it to spring up,
So the Lord GOD will cause righteousness and praise
To spring up before all the nations. (Is. 61:10–11)

Thus says the Lord GOD, "I shall also take a sprig from the lofty top of the cedar and set it out; I shall pluck from the topmost of its young twigs a tender one, and I shall plant it on a high and lofty mountain. On the high mountain of Israel I shall plant it, that it may bring forth boughs and bear fruit, and become a stately cedar. And birds of every kind will nest under it; they will nest in the shade of its branches. And all the trees of the field will know that I am the LORD; I bring down the high tree, exalt the low tree, dry up the green tree, and make the dry tree flourish. I am the LORD; I have spoken, and I will perform it." (Ezek. 17:22–24)

Therefore, prophesy concerning the land of Israel, and say to the mountains and to the hills, to the ravines and to the valleys, "Thus says the Lord GOD, 'Behold, I have spoken in My jealousy and in My wrath because you have endured the insults of the nations.' Therefore, thus says the Lord GOD, 'I have sworn that surely the nations which are around you will themselves endure their insults. But you, O mountains of Israel, you will put forth your branches and bear your fruit for My people Israel; for they will soon come. For, behold, I am for you, and I will turn to you, and you shall be cultivated and sown. And I will multiply men on you, all the house of Israel, all of it; and the cities will be inhabited, and the waste places will be rebuilt. And I will multiply on you man and beast; and they will increase and be fruitful; and I will cause you to be inhabited as you were formerly and will treat you better than at the first. Thus you will know that I am the LORD.'" (Ezek. 36:6–11)

Israel has been planted, but the seed has gone bad. Jesus finds different groups now in Israel whom He explains by using the analogy of varying soils. Some have simply become barren ground. That is the first kind of soil. Some may bear thirty, sixty, or a hundredfold. That is Jesus Himself and perhaps a few others whom Jesus meets along the way who demonstrate faith.

The more interesting soils are the second and third kinds. Jesus was in danger from the plots of the Pharisees and the Herodians. Furthermore, He has in His own company those zealous to make Him king and unwilling to contemplate the cross as the proper place for the king, as well as one who might forget about the Kingdom for the sake of thirty pieces of silver. The second soil corresponds to the Pharisees, the Zealots, and the disciples who want Him to reject the cross. The third soil is the Herodians and Sadducees and the one disciple who, at the final hour, is in it for the money.

THE SHALLOW SOIL

Jesus states that the growth from the seed in the second soil represents those who "fall away" under persecution. This is precisely how Jesus describes the impending behavior of His own disciples when He is about to be arrested at Gethsemane: "You will all fall away" (Mk. 14:27). These soils are not unchangeable characterizations of people, nor are the first three types of soil meant to represent different types of unregenerate hearts. The fact is that, as we are moved from glory to glory, we continually must struggle to respond to the Word of God in a manner pleasing to God. The parable of the soils should be taken as an exhortation to *those who are Christians* to continually repent and believe.

When Jesus was seized, one of His followers attacked the mob with his sword and only succeeded in cutting the ear of the high priest's servant (14:47). Jesus' parable actually addresses this sort of hot-headed zeal: "And other seed fell on the rocky ground where it did not have much soil; and immediately it sprang up *because it had no depth of soil*" (Mk. 4:5; emphasis added). The same condition in the soil, which causes it to wither under persecution, is also the reason why there is such a sudden and visible response to the message of the Kingdom.

> And in a similar way these are the ones on whom seed was sown on the rocky places, who, when they hear the word, immediately receive it with joy; and they have no firm root in themselves, but are only temporary; then, when affliction or persecution arises because of the word, immediately they fall away. (Mk. 4:16–17)

Why is persecution associated with this group? Because they are zealous for the message of the Kingdom, they seek out trouble. For the third soil persecution is not an issue. Rather they are those who find in the Kingdom material comforts and cease believing the Word. The Sadducees, as Mark will later tell us, no longer believed in the resurrection. In their view the Kingdom did not need to come. They were content with the way things were (with themselves in control of the priesthood by the backing of the Romans). Judas himself falls into this trap. Once it becomes clear that Jesus is on a virtual "suicide mission," he decides that preserving his own life and gaining a little something for the future are more important than the hope of the Kingdom.

DARK SAYINGS: SECRECY & REVELATION (4:21–25)

Having explained the parable of the soils, Jesus goes on to tell a parable about the responsibility of the disciples to clearly explain His parables at some point in the future. Jesus' secrecy is temporary. Eventually the disciples will be held responsible to relate publicly everything Jesus teaches them in private.

DARK SAYINGS: THE SEED (4:26–34)

Jesus finishes up with two parables of growth, which take up the subject of the fourth soil in the parable of the soils. All He said then was that there would be prodigious fruitfulness. Now He elaborates in two ways. In the parable of the man sowing seed, He emphasizes how the Kingdom comes and grows and reaches ripeness for the harvest without any intervention on the part of man. In the parable about the Mustard Seed, Jesus leaves aside *how* the kingdom will grow and takes up the question of *how much* it will grow. His answer is that it will grow into a world empire. This is reference to several Old Testament passages, most clearly to Ezekiel 17:23, but also to such passages as Daniel 4, in which Nebuchadnezzar was portrayed as a huge tree that was cut down because of pride. Jesus is saying that the Kingdom will grow and expand until it is more than Nebuchadnezzar dreamed of, but that it will never be cut down.

THE WAVES TOSS (4:35–41)

Jesus told His disciples that to them was given to know the mysteries of the Kingdom. Now, just before they get into the boat, Mark reiterates this fact by mentioning that Jesus was only giving the crowd parables, but was explaining the parables to the disciples.

Yet now, in the boat, Jesus questions their faith. This is our first hint that it is not only the Pharisees or the crowds who, while seeing may see and not perceive and while hearing may hear and not understand.

"Hear this, O foolish and senseless people,
Who have eyes, but see not;
Who have ears, but hear not.
Do you not fear Me?" declares the LORD. "Do you not tremble in
My presence?

For I have placed the sand as a boundary for the sea,
An eternal decree, so it cannot cross over it.
Though the waves toss, yet they cannot prevail;
Though they roar, yet they cannot cross over it.
But this people has a stubborn and rebellious heart;
They have turned aside and departed.
They do not say in their heart, 'Let us now fear the LORD our God,
Who gives rain in its season,
Both the autumn rain and the spring rain,
Who keeps for us
The appointed weeks of the harvest.'" (Jer. 5:21–24)

"Who then is this, that even the wind and sea obey him?" Not understanding the parables is bound up in not understanding or fearing the Lord and not understanding Jesus. The disciples themselves have blind eyes and hard hearts.

THE DROWNING OF THE ARMY (5:1–20)

Jesus said that He had bound the strong man. Now, in the first exorcism story since the first restoration in chapter 1,[2] He meets a man whom no one can bind, and yet He tames him with a word. Of course, the demons are not really the strong man but rather multitudes of his army. "Legion" is a military term for a great number of soldiers.

Why did Jesus allow this demonic army to go into a herd of swine? He undoubtedly wanted to teach His disciples. Jesus had just brought them through the sea by a miracle and now He drives a demonic horde into that same sea to drown them. Like Moses at

---

[2] Noting the similarity in the Greek word for Spirit (which also means "breath" and "wind"), Austin Farrer points out that the calming of the storm with the exorcism of Legion looks like a doubled refiguring of the synagogue exorcism in chapter 1 of Mark's Gospel (85, 86):

> And just then there was in their synagogue a man with an unclean spirit; and he cried out, saying, "What do we have to do with You, Jesus of Nazareth? **Have You come to destroy us?** I know who You are—the Holy One of God!" **And Jesus** rebuked him, **saying,** "Be quiet, and come out of him!" And throwing him into convulsions, the unclean spirit cried out with a loud voice, and came out of him. And **they were all amazed, so that they debated among themselves, saying, "What is this? A new teaching with authority! He commands even the unclean spirits, and they obey**

the Red Sea, the enemy army is destroyed by the very means God uses to transport His people across the water. The lesson, for anyone reflecting on these two signs working together, would be that the *real* enemy is Satan's host. For first-century Palestinian Jews, the story of God's deliverance of Israel from Pharaoh's army would most easily translate into expectant prayer and hope that God would deliver Israel from the Romans. But Jesus' miracle gives a slightly different application.

Not only does Jesus deliver the man from his demons, but he also sends him to witness to the Gentiles. It seems that Jesus did not have the same worries about the news of him spreading in that region, outside of Israel where He was mainly ministering.

THE TWO DEAD DAUGHTERS (5:21–43)

Jesus is now back by the seashore. We have already seen calling by the sea turn into calling by teaching by the sea (Mk. 4:1). Now we find a new perspective on what Jesus is doing. If He is going to call people or teach them, He is going to have to raise them from the dead. As we see in Jesus sending the man once possessed by Legion to testify about Him, when God calls us, He is ultimately calling us out of the graveyard.

Mark once again sandwiches two events so they can interpret one another. He begins with a father asking help for his daughter who is at death's door (v. 23). Then another woman interrupts them on their way, to whom Jesus refers as "Daughter" (v. 34). The

---

Him." And immediately <u>the news about Him went out everywhere into all the surrounding district of Galilee</u> .(Mk. 1:23–28)

And there arose a fierce gale of wind, and the waves were breaking over the boat so much that the boat was already filling up. And He Himself was in the stern, asleep on the cushion; and they awoke Him and said to Him, "Teacher, **do You not care that we are perishing?**" And being aroused, **He rebuked the wind** and said to the sea, "Hush, **be still.**" And the wind died down and it became perfectly calm. And He said to them, "Why are you so timid? How is it that you have no faith?" And **they became very much afraid and said to one another, "Who then is this, that even the wind and the sea obey Him?"** (Mk. 4:37–41)

woman has been suffering, Mark tells us, for twelve years (Mk. 5:25). When Jesus raises Jairus' daughter, we learn that she is twelve years old (v. 42). Plainly, Mark wants us to associate these two people.

THE WOMAN WITH THE ISSUE OF BLOOD

The case of a woman who can't stop bleeding from her menstrual flow is directly addressed in the Bible.

> Now if a woman has a discharge of her blood many days, not at the period of her menstrual impurity, or if she has a discharge beyond that period, all the days of her impure discharge she shall continue as though in her menstrual impurity; she is unclean. Any bed on which she lies all the days of her discharge shall be to her like her bed at menstruation; and every thing on which she sits shall be unclean, like her uncleanness at that time. Likewise, whoever touches them shall be unclean and shall wash his clothes and bathe in water and be unclean until evening. (Lev. 15:25–27)

What this basically means is that, under the Mosaic system, a woman menstruating could make anything into the ceremonial equivalent of a carcass simply by coming into contact with it.

> If one of the animals dies which you have for food, the one who touches its carcass becomes unclean until evening. He too, who eats some of its carcass shall wash his clothes and be unclean until evening; and the one who picks up its carcass shall wash his clothes and be unclean until evening. (Lev. 11:39–40)

Thus, we see here that the problem with the woman with the issue of blood is, according to Leviticus, a problem of ceremonial

---

And when He had come out of the boat, <u>immediately a man from the tombs with an unclean spirit met Him</u>, and he had his dwelling among the tombs. And no one was able to bind him anymore, even with a chain; because he had often been bound with shackles and chains, and the chains had been torn apart by him, and the shackles broken in pieces, and no one was strong enough to subdue him. And constantly night and day, among the tombs and in the mountains, he was crying out and gashing himself with stones. And seeing Jesus from a distance, he ran up and bowed down before Him; and <u>crying out with a loud voice, he said, "What do I have to do with You, Jesus, Son of the Most High God</u>? I implore You by God, do not torment me!" For <u>He had been saying to him, "Come out of the man</u>, you unclean spirit!" And He was asking him, "What is your name?" And he said to Him, "My name is Legion; for we are many." And death. Furthermore, this is much more than a mere medical problem. For twelve years this woman had been barred from participating in the annual sacramental meals of the Old Covenant: Passover, Pentecost, the Feast of Booths. She cannot even approach Jerusalem in her unclean condition. Ultimately, death is not a biological problem, but rather an alienation from God. Until this woman is healed and cleansed, she is exiled from the presence of God.

Why did she think that merely touching the hem of Jesus' robe would bring her healing and cleansing? According to the Levitical system, she had no business, as an unclean person, touching anyone (which is probably why she trembled when she publicly confessed what she had done). Yet she not only touched Him, but also had confidence that He would heal her without even knowing about her. We know from Jesus' own testimony that the woman was showing "faith" that "saved" her (Mk. 5:34). But how is this act not superstitious?

If the woman knew anything of Jesus' ministry, she knew (1) that Jesus touched unclean people (2) without becoming unclean Himself, and, in so doing, (3) cleansed those who were unclean. She inferred from this that the principles of uncleanness from Leviticus did not operate in the case of Jesus. To see how these principles would normally operate, consider God's questioning of the priests:

> On the twenty-fourth of the ninth month, in the second year of Darius, the word of the LORD came to Haggai the prophet saying,

---

he began to entreat Him earnestly not to send them out of the country. Now there was a big herd of swine feeding there on the mountain. And the demons entreated Him, saying, "Send us into the swine so that we may enter them." And He gave them permission. And coming out, the unclean spirits entered the swine; and the herd rushed down the steep bank into the sea, about two thousand of them; and they were drowned in the sea . . . And he went away and began to proclaim in Decapolis what great things Jesus had done for him; and everyone marveled. (Mk. 5:2–12, 20)

The next miracle in Mark 1 is the raising of Simon's mother-in-law, which is recorded in a way to be doubly refigured in the cleansing of the woman with the issue of blood and raising of Jairus' daughter (also done in a family home and at the behest of a family member).

"Thus says the LORD of hosts, 'Ask now the priests for a ruling: If a man carries holy meat in the fold of his garment, and touches bread with this fold, or cooked food, wine, oil, or any other food, will it become holy?'" And the priests answered and said, "No." Then Haggai said, "If one who is unclean from a corpse touches any of these, will the latter become unclean?" And the priests answered and said, "It will become unclean." (Hag. 2:10–13)

Under the Mosaic system Death spread but Life did not. But Death was not a problem for Jesus. Death was not drawn into Him. Uncleanness did not spread to Him.

Jesus, on the other hand, spread cleansing life out of Himself. In fact, the woman is confident that cleanliness will spread from Jesus in exactly the way it normally would *not* spread from a sanctified object. Jesus' own body is the holy meat and the fringe of His garment is the fold carrying the meat. But she is sure she *will* be sanctified by simply coming into contact with the garment that is in contact with Jesus. Even before His resurrection, Jesus is a source of life and health.

THE GIRL WHO WAS DEAD

As the source of life, Jesus is ultimately out to accomplish not merely healing, but full resurrection. All other problems are simply manifestations beforehand of death. All healings are therefore pointers to the promise of resurrection. Mark tells us just enough about the raising of Jairus' daughter to present it as the fulfillment of all the previous healings. As in the case of the synagogue demon, Jesus does what He can to keep this work a secret, and those who do look on are amazed. As in the case of Simon's mother-in-law, here again we have a person interceding on behalf of a family relation; Jesus again takes a woman by the hand and raises her up, and afterwards there is a meal. As in the case of the leper, Jesus touches one who is unclean. As in the case of the paralytic, one who cannot move suddenly begins to walk at Jesus' authoritative command. As in the case of the withered hand, Jesus heals despite unbelief and commands the recipient to "arise."

The most recent restoration miracles are even more closely related to the raising of Jairus' daughter. In the case of the woman with the issue of blood, we have already mentioned that the two cases are sandwiched together and that both women are called "daughter" and they each have twelve years. But even in the case of the Gerasene demoniac, we see Mark preparing us for this miracle of resurrection. The demons possessing this wretch were not only "unclean" (Mk. 5:2), but they forced him to inhabit "the tombs" (v. 5). Could Mark come closer to portraying the salvation of a man as resurrection from the dead without actually giving us a literal resurrection? Mark has been building up all along from lesser healing to greater in order to climax with Jairus' daughter whom He does literally rescue from death. Jesus is the resurrection and the life.

This is the first resurrection in Mark's Gospel. The second resurrection and final healing will be that of Jesus. How is Mark going to be able to continue heightening his record of Jesus' victories? Once Jairus' daughter is raised, he changes the sorts of miracles he tells us about in order to keep heightening the story. Before, he has told us of Jesus healing those who cannot walk about or of him restoring a withered hand. Afterwards, he tells us of the restoration of deaf-mutes and blind men. We cease to read of any restorations of men or women who are bedridden or who have damaged limbs or torsos. Luke tells us that Jesus straightened out a woman with a crooked back, but Mark reports only head problems. Everything changes after the first resurrection.

The last thing said in this paragraph is that Jesus tells her parents to give the girl something to eat. There is no reason to think that Jesus has exhausted His power with raising a corpse and cannot provide the necessary nutrition to eliminate her hunger. If Jesus has raised her with a need for food, He has done so for significant reasons. Jesus' eating and drinking has already gained notoriety. Jesus is restoring people to table fellowship. Having been admitted into new life, Jairus' daughter displays that God raises us up to give us table fellowship. Given Mark's association of calling with restoration, we see here baptism and then Eucharist.

RESURRECTION TO REJECTION (6:1–6)

We come to the end of a cycle in Mark. Jesus is about to summon the Twelve to fulfill their calling and go on a mission (6:7–13). We should remember that Jesus went about "preaching the gospel of God" (Mk. 1:14–15) right before He called the first four disciples (1:16–20). Then He went to the seashore teaching the multitude (Mk. 2:13) right before He called Levi (2:14). Then He taught and healed many (Mk. 3:7–12) right before He called the Twelve (3:13–19). Now that we are coming upon a new but different calling, we would expect another episode of teaching and healing.

Jesus seems to have a similar expectation, for He goes to His hometown in order to teach and heal. Having performed the greatest miracle of Mark's Gospel up to now, Jesus returns to His own only to be rejected. Whereas Jairus and his wife were "completely astounded" (Mk. 5:42), now it is Jesus' turn to "wonder," this time "at their unbelief" (Mk. 6:6).

The resurrection of Jairus' daughter gives us a hint of what will happen at the second resurrection in Mark's gospel. It too will be followed by unbelief.

Mark 6:7–9:1

Calling & Eucharist

J esus has already established that He calls (and restores) sinners in order to dine with them around the table. However,
while the emphasis before the raising of Jairus' daughter
emphasized the healing and forgiveness, now we will find
Mark especially showing that Jesus is the ultimate King and
banquet master. He is not only able and willing to feed the world,
both Israel and the nations, but He is in the process of inviting all
to His new feast.

SENDING THE TWELVE (6:7–13)

Jesus, once again, calls His disciples. This time, Mark does not explicitly mention the sea being nearby. He has reserved such associations for His initial calling of men to be His disciples. Nevertheless, the sending of the Twelve on a mission reminds the reader
of the whole point of calling the Twelve on that mountain by the
sea.

> And He went up to the mountain and summoned those whom He
> Himself wanted, and they came to Him. And He appointed twelve,
> that they might be with Him, and that He might send them out to
> preach, and to have authority to cast out the demons. And He
> appointed the twelve. (Mk. 3:13–16)

> And He summoned the twelve and began to send them out in pairs;
> and He was giving them authority over the unclean spirits.... And
> they went out and preached that men should repent. And they were
> casting out many demons and were anointing with oil many sick
> people and healing them. (Mk. 6:7, 12–13)

What we see here is a movement from promise to fulfillment.
The purpose for which Jesus chose the Twelve is now being realized.

In trying to understand Jesus' ministry in its context, we also find here an important factor that must be considered: No matter how much His disciples misunderstood Jesus, they must have understood His basic message well enough to proclaim it on His behalf as His representatives. Any interpretation of Jesus' message, that turns it into something completely foreign to the thinking of Jesus' contemporaries needs to be regarded with suspicion. Such a criterion would help us not fall for simplistic slogans such as, "Jesus preached a spiritual kingdom [i.e. a non-material Kingdom], not a political or physical kingdom like the Jews were expecting." It is true that Jesus did not see the geo-political markers of the kingdom as having permanent standing. But He nevertheless was re-organizing a people as a new Israel throughout His ministry. A body of people marked out by new ceremonies and new duties of thought and life is a material, physical reality, even if it is no longer bound by geographical borders or civic authority. We will only understand the revolutionary nature of what He was doing if we consider it from the perspective of the background of the Old Testament Scriptures.

THE MINISTRY & ITS SUPPORT

While a special mission of the Twelve seems like a rather unique event, the New Testament indicates that this is one of the most applicable and practical stories in the synoptic Gospels. For here we see the beginning of the ministry of the Church. What Mark tells us was given to the Twelve, Luke reveals was also given to seventy others. Paul then takes the principles set down in these accounts and finds rules for pastors or evangelists in the Church (1 Cor. 9:14; 1 Tim. 5:18).

> ...and He instructed them that they should take nothing for their journey, except a mere staff; no bread, no bag, no money in their belt; but to wear sandals; and He added, "Do not put on two tunics." And He said to them, "Wherever you enter a house, stay there until you leave town. And any place that does not receive you or listen to you, as you go out from there, shake off the dust from the soles of your feet for a testimony against them." (Mk. 6:8–11)

First, let's see how these directives may apply today to others beside the original group of Twelve to whom Jesus was speaking, and then let's consider what those directives mean for them.

Parallel accounts are found in Matthew 10:1–15 and Luke 9:1–5. Matthew's longer account includes as one of Jesus' sayings at this time, "The worker is worthy of his nourishment" (Mk. 10:10b). Luke omits this statement in his brief recounting of the sending of the Twelve. But Luke also tells us that Jesus sent out seventy (10:1–16) and gave them the same principle: "The laborer is worthy of his wages" (Mk. 10:7b).

Commonly, Jesus' exhortation not to wear two tunics is treated as a mandate for pastors to not be concerned as to whether they are being adequately supported. In fact, it is a mandate for congregations to provide their pastors with adequate support. Jesus is telling the disciples not to spend their own savings on this assignment, but rather expect to be maintained as long as the mission lasts.

In his letter to the Corinthians, we see Paul appealing to the saying of Jesus that a worker is worthy of his wages:

> My defense to those who examine me is this: Do we not have a right to eat and drink? Do we not have a right to take along a believing wife, even as the rest of the apostles, and the brothers of the Lord, and Cephas? Or do only Barnabas and I not have a right to refrain from working? Who at any time serves as a soldier at his own expense? Who plants a vineyard, and does not eat the fruit of it? Or who tends a flock and does not use the milk of the flock? I am not speaking these things according to human judgment, am I? Or does not the Law also say these things? For it is written in the Law of Moses, "You shall not muzzle the ox while he is threshing" [Deut. 25:4]. God is not concerned about oxen, is He? Or is He speaking altogether for our sake? Yes, for our sake it was written, because the plowman ought to plow in hope, and the thresher to thresh in hope of sharing the crops. If we sowed spiritual things in you, is it too much if we should reap material things from you? If others share the right over you, do we not more? Nevertheless, we did not use this right, but we endure all things, that we may cause no hindrance to the gospel of Christ. Do you not know that those who perform sacred services eat the food of the temple, and those who attend regularly to the altar have their share with the altar? *So also the Lord directed those who proclaim the gospel to get their living from the gospel.* But I have used none of these things. And I am not writing these things that it may be done so in my case; for it would be better for me to die than have any man make my boast an empty one. (1 Cor. 9:3–15; emphasis added)

Paul revisits this issue again when writing to Timothy:

> Let the presbyters "elders" who rule well be considered worthy of double honor, especially those who toil in word and instruction. For the Scripture says, "You shall not muzzle the ox while he is threshing," and "The laborer is worthy of his wages." (1 Tim. 5:17–18)

John Calvin saw in this passage reference not only to pastors but also to other rulers in the Church whom Reformed believers now commonly call "ruling elders."[1] There is no proof available, however, that Paul is talking in 1 Timothy 5:17–18 about ruling elders and pastors in Presbyterian polity. He could just as well be speaking of pastors known for their counseling or administrative gifts versus those known for their preaching and teaching. Or he could be speaking of pastors in charge of established congregations versus evangelists.[2]

Whatever the case, we have in Mark 6:7–13 the beginnings not merely of the temporary apostolate, but of the perpetual office of minister or pastor, which is developed before our very eyes as we read the rest of the New Testament. Mark is typically brief in his recounting of the event, but we can still notice that these men are chosen to *represent* Jesus because they are sent to speak and do what Jesus has been speaking and doing. Matthew records that Jesus clearly stated this to the Twelve: "He who receives you receives Me, and he who receives Me receives Him who sent Me" (Mt. 10:40). Luke tells us that such authority was not limited to the Twelve but included seventy others: "The one who listens to you listens to Me, and the one who rejects you rejects Me; and he who rejects Me rejects the One who sent Me" (Lk. 10:16). John reveals that Jesus repeated this commission after His resurrection and before His ascension:

---

[1] "In the Epistle to Timothy, also, he mentions two kinds of presbyters, some who labour in the word, and others who do not perform the office of preaching, but rule well (1 Tim. 5:17)" (*Institutes*, Beveridge, tr., IV. 11. 1.).

[2] The problem with Calvin's understanding is that such officers have never been supported full-time and could not be supported full-time in most congregations. 1 Corinthians 9 tells us that the office of minister is normally one which involves full-time pay. If ministers of the Gospel and unpaid lay rulers in the church both held one office, then no one could question the Apostle Paul's office on the basis that he did not receive compensation for his work. He would simply be doing what the majority of the men did who held his office.

When therefore it was evening, on that day, the first day of the week, and when the doors were shut where the disciples were, for fear of the Jews, Jesus came and stood in their midst, and said to them, "Peace be with you." And when He had said this, He showed them both His hands and His side. The disciples therefore rejoiced when they saw the Lord. Jesus therefore said to them again, "Peace be with you; *as the Father has sent Me, I also send you.*" And when He had said this, He breathed on them, and said to them, "Receive the Holy Spirit. If you forgive the sins of any, their sins have been forgiven them; if you retain the sins of any, they have been retained." (Jn. 20:19–23; emphasis added)

John's inclusion of the power to forgive sins in the commission of the disciples should not surprise us. Mark has already shown Jesus claiming that His power to miraculously heal was proof of His power to forgive (Mk. 2:9–12). If Jesus is now giving the power of exorcism and healing to His disciples, then we know that the power to forgive is not far behind. Thus, it has been the common practice throughout the ages, including during and after the Protestant Reformation, for pastors to lead their congregations in a corporate confession of sin and then to declare to them their forgiveness.

ANOINTING WITH OIL

Mark alone of all the Gospel writers tells us that the disciples "were anointing with oil many sick people and healing them" (Mk. 6:13). This is a strange use of oil. Anointing was done, according to the Hebrew Scriptures, to install a person into an office—as David was anointed by Samuel. It was never used specifically for healing. Jesus must have taught His disciples to perform this rite, and we need to think about why He did so.

Mark shows us Jesus giving to His disciples His authority and power to heal and to cast out demons to His disciples. We see that Jesus as the Son of Man is able to share His royal perogatives with His subjects. And now, by anointing others, the disciples are extending Jesus' royal calling as the Christ, the Anointed One, to others. Years later the Apostle Paul writes, "Now he who establishes us with you in Christ and anointed us is God." "Christ" and "anointed" are the same root word and Paul is obviously using them so close together in order to relate them (in the Greek: *eis Christon kai chrisas*). When we are put in Christ, we are anointed in His anointing. The disciples are putting the sick into solidarity with Jesus the Anointed One.

We have already mentioned in chapter 3 that the sons of Aaron could not serve as priests if they had a defect of any kind or were unclean (Lev. 21:16–22:4). Introducing this prohibition is a statement about the special requirements of the High Priest that especially involve the oil of his anointing.

> And the priest who is the highest among his brothers, on whose head the anointing oil has been poured, and who has been consecrated to wear the garments, shall not uncover his head, nor tear his clothes; nor shall he approach any dead person, nor defile himself even for his father or his mother; nor shall he go out of the sanctuary, nor profane the sanctuary of his God; for the consecration of the anointing oil of his God is on him: I am the LORD. (Lev. 21:10–12)

While these requirements are not established for kings, they do point to the more general requirement that when one is anointed for an office, it is assumed that he can perform the tasks to which he is being assigned. David, at his anointing, "was ruddy, with beautiful eyes and a handsome appearance" (1 Sam. 16:12). Why would one anoint a sick person?

The answer has to lie in the vocation of Jesus himself. The disciples are anointing those who are sick and then the sick are becoming healthy. Jesus is anointed to die, and after death He will come to new life.

This should help us understand what is happening when the church elders anoint the sick, and yet they are not healed (Jas. 5:14–16). While we do hope that our sick brothers and sisters will be healed, this does not mean that the anointing has not "worked" unless they recover their health. The main point of anointing is calling to a task. We anoint our sick to formally call them to suffer and rise in union with Jesus Christ who died and was raised to new life. If God does not raise them up in temporary health (this side of the grave all health is temporary), then He will raise them up at the Last Day. By anointing those suffering with sickness, we officially ordain them to show forth the Gospel—the life and death and new life of Christ—in their own persons.

THE FEAST OF THE CANNIBAL KING (6:14–29)

Having sent the twelve on a mission, Mark finds it appropriate to include a rather lengthy recap of the martyrdom of John the Baptist. Feasting has been established as an important aspect of Jesus' ministry. Here we see Satan's counterfeit—a feast where the saints are on the menu. John's head on a platter is not simply a gruesome detail; it also establishes King Herod as the opposite of the greater King David. Jesus is the good shepherd who lays down His life for His sheep. For Herod his flock is simply livestock to supply his table.

If Jesus is comparable to Elijah (Mk. 6:15), then how could Herod and Herodias fail to correspond to Ahab and Jezebel? Like Ahab on occasion, Herod seems almost like a "nice guy," since he wants to protect John, and Herodias is the one who is out to kill him. If Mark wants to make such a point, then he is showing us why it was important for Jesus to repudiate His natural family (Mk. 3:31–35) and is also showing the basis for even more severe statements to come (Mk. 13:12). If Herod had not made his own sinful family, as well as his dinner guests, more important in his eyes than the life of a righteous man, he might have been able to repent and believe. Instead, for all his interest in John, he remained in his sins.

THE TYPOLOGY OF JOHN'S MARTYRDOM

It is no accident that Mark just happens to mention John's fate at this point in his Gospel. The preceding three stories set the stage. Jesus performed His first and only resurrection in Mark's Gospel (5:35–43), was rejected by His own people (6:1–6), and gave the Twelve a commission—not the Great Commission yet, but still a commission! Here in the middle of Jesus' ministry we have the elements of its end and new beginning.

Our new passage begins with a response: "And King Herod heard . . ." Heard about *what*? Mark tells us that Jesus' name had become well-known (Mk. 6:14), but the context demands that we associate Jesus' fame with the immediately preceding verse. It is the miraculous power and preaching being seen in Jesus' twelve disciples that is making Jesus well-known. In response then to the miracles performed by the disciples, some infer that Jesus must be his predecessor:"John the Baptist has risen from the dead, and that is why these miraculous powers are at work in Him."

Herod and others are mistaken, but they are using valid principles for interpreting what they are seeing in their midst. According to the last verse of the "longer ending" of Mark's gospel, the disciples "went out and preached everywhere, *while the Lord worked with them* and confirmed the word by the signs that followed" (Mk. 16:20). Resurrection means new power displayed through others. Inasmuch as Jesus is John's successor, Herod is not entirely wrong. John's martyrdom, his willingness to become less that Jesus might be more, is in an important sense a factor that made possible Jesus' present ministry with His chosen disciples.

In the context of guesses about John's resurrection and the resulting "Great Commission," the details Mark relates concerning John's death are rather intriguing. John was the prisoner of a man who did not want to put him to death. But at a special banquet others connived to trick Herod into promising to kill him. Herod is not only Ahab from the past, but Pilate in the future. His birthday celebration corresponds to the Passover, his promise to Herodias' daughter to Pilate's custom of releasing a prisoner. Herodias plays the part of the chief priests and scribes. John as Jesus' predecessor prefigures his death.

The main difference is that John's disciples don't abandon him, but bury his body (Mk. 6:29). Jesus dies alone and is buried by others.

THE FEAST OF THE GOOD SHEPHERD ON GREEN PASTURES (6:30–44)

The first question is: Why should Mark feel the need to inform us that the grass on which the people sat was green?

> The LORD is my shepherd
> I shall not want.
> He makes me lie down in green pastures. (Ps. 23.1–2a)

And since the next event will be the walking on the water and the calming of the storm:

> He leads me beside waters of rest. (Ps. 23.2b)

The prophets foretold that God would send David to be a king and shepherd to his people (Ezek. 34:23; 37:24). But David insisted that Yahweh (a.k.a. "the LORD" in our English translations) was his Shepherd. Here we see the two statements converging as the heir of David acts as God the Shepherd does according to David's Psalm by making his sheep recline on the green pastures. For He has compassion on them, seeing that they are like sheep without a shepherd (Mk. 6:34).

They need someone better than Herod.

BREAKING BREAD

Jesus merely apportions or alots the fish, but the bread He literally *breaks* just as He will do later at His last Passover (Mk. 14:22). Miraculous bread is more than sufficient for the needs of God's flock. David, as Jesus reminded the scribes earlier (Mk. 2:25–26), had to go to the Tabernacle in order to gain five loaves for his men (1 Sam. 21:3). But the greater David is able to take five loaves and feed five thousand with twelve containers of leftovers. This is a miraculous foreshadowing of the Lord's Supper.

Once again we see Mark's pattern surfacing, and find that he has taken a theme with small beginnings and allowed it to grow to greatness as we read his Gospel. After calling Simon, Andrew, James, and John, Jesus went to Simon's house and raised up his mother-in-law so that she could wait on their table. After calling Levi, Jesus went to his house and ate and drank at a banquet with all his friends. After calling the Twelve, He returned to Simon's house to attempt to eat, but was unable due to the overwhelming crowd. Here we find the same situation—a calling and then a feasting. In fact, here we find the last situation reduplicated: Jesus and His disciples are too overwhelmed to eat bread because of the Twelve (Mk. 3:20; 6:31). This time, however, Jesus is not going to stand for it. He shows that He can, by the power of the Spirit, meet the needs of a great host. Here we have a new level of emphasis on Jesus' ministry of eating and drinking. While at first He had been content to call people to a "natural" feast, now He reveals the full import of His dining with sinners by providing supernatural bread. He who has been relying on others such as Simon's mother-in-law or Levi to feed him now shows that He has the resources to be the host and provider in abundance.

Jesus does not suddenly institute the sacrament of the Lord's Supper "out of the blue" in chapter 14. Rather, we see that He is building up to it in Mark's gospel from the beginning of His ministry.

TWELVE FULL BASKETS FROM FIVE LOAVES, FOR FIVE THOUSAND

Since Jesus will explicitly refer to this later (Mk. 8:17–21), we need to ask ourselves the significance of the numbers. The twelve remaining are not hard to figure out. They correspond to the twelve tribes of Israel—signifying perhaps that even after feeding this host, Jesus has the power to restore all Israel if they would believe in him.

The five loaves for five thousand may seem more difficult, but I would suggest that this too is a number especially to be associated with Israel. Before God fed the Israelites with the bread of heaven, He led them out of Egypt "in battle array" (Exod. 13:18; NASB) or "in orderly ranks" (NKJV) but literally "five in a rank." Marching by fives was a military formation, and it is how God organized Israel to leave Egypt.[3] Since the wilderness is also the place where Israel was restructured with judges "of thousands, of hundreds, of fifties, and of tens" (Exod. 18:25), Mark's reference to the five thousand men plus women and children reclining "in companies of hundreds and fifties" (Mk. 6:40) would reinforce this allusion to Israel in the wilderness.

This is Israel's feast. With the one exception of the Gerasene demoniac in the region of the Decapolis, Jesus' ministry has been centered on Israel. Indeed, the last miracle He performed was the resurrection of the synagogue ruler's daughter at his request. Later Mark will present us with a different daughter healed in response to the request of a different kind of parent followed by a meal designed for a different group of people.

[3] C.f Matthew Henry's comments on this passage.

BY THE STILL WATERS (6:45–56)

Why is it that Jesus "intended to pass by" His disciples? Perhaps they were supposed to see Him and be reassured that they were being cared for even in the midst of the storm. The last time Jesus was in a storm with them, He was asleep and seemed not to care. This time, He is awake and demonstrating His power over the wind and the waves. But if Jesus was trying to reassure the Twelve, His plan backfired and they became more afraid than ever. Jesus is always more terrifying than nature.

The difference, however, is that while before, His disciples were terrified at His saving them, now they are terrified that He is a harbinger of death to them. We noticed at the first storm at sea that there were indications in Jeremiah (Mk. 5:21–24) that it was not only the scribes who were unable to perceive and had hardened hearts. Now Mark tells us that, despite the provision made through the loaves, the disciples had gained no insight because "their heart was hardened" (Mk. 6:52).

THE ANGEL OF THE LORD

The first time Jesus miraculously brought His disciples through the sea, He destroyed a demonic army in those waters. This, we observed, presents Jesus as the Lord leading a new Israel on a new Exodus. If we allow that Mark has thus established that sea-crossings have such significance, then we find here some interesting parallels. After Jesus crossed the sea we read:

> And when they had come out of the boat, immediately *the people* recognized Him, and ran about that whole country and began to carry about on their pallets those who were sick, to the place they heard He was. And wherever He entered villages, or cities, or countryside, they were laying the sick in the market places, and entreating Him that they might just touch the fringe of His cloak; and as many as touched it were being cured. (Mk. 6:54–56)

After the Israelites crossed the Red Sea we read:

> Then Moses led Israel from the Red Sea, and they went out into the wilderness of Shur; and they went three days in the wilderness and found no water. And when they came to Marah, they could

not drink the waters of Marah, for they were bitter; therefore it was named Marah. So the people grumbled at Moses, saying, "What shall we drink?" Then he cried out to the LORD, and the LORD showed him a tree; and he threw it into the waters, and the waters became sweet. There He made for them a statute and regulation, and there He tested them. And He said, "If you will give earnest heed to the voice of the LORD your God, and do what is right in His sight, and give ear to His commandments, and keep all His statutes, I will put none of the diseases on you which I have put on the Egyptians; for I, the LORD, am your healer." (Exod. 15:22–26)

Jesus is their healer now, just as He was their healer then.

HOLINESS & THE HEART (7:1–23)

For the second time we find scribes and Pharisees from Jerusalem journeying to accuse Jesus (7:1; 3:22). Since Jesus has recently fed multitudes in a significant way, the leaders attempt to discredit His ability as a host. If His disciples don't care about purity in their eating bread, how dare any righteous Israelite receive bread from His hands. Just as, formerly, the scribes from Jerusalem used the mention of His madness and exorcisms to formulate an accusation about His deal with the devil, (3:20–35) so it is now. The last miracle reported by Mark is that Jesus was allowing the sick (presumably the unclean) to touch him. Thus, the Pharisaical accusation encompasses both food and cleanliness.

WOE TO JERUSALEM

Jesus does not hold back in His response to these representatives from Jerusalem. He quotes Isaiah 29:13, the conclusion of a prophecy of judgment on a specific city.

> Woe, O Ariel, Ariel the city where David once camped!
> Add year to year, observe your feasts on schedule.
> And I will bring distress to Ariel,
> And she shall be a city of lamenting and mourning;
> And she shall be like an Ariel to me.
> And I will camp against you encircling you,
> And I will set siegeworks against you,
> And I will raise up battle towers against you.

Then you shall be brought low;
From the earth you shall speak,
And from the dust where you are prostrate,
Your words shall come.
Your voice shall also be like that of a spirit from the ground,
And your speech shall whisper from the dust.
But the multitude of your enemies shall become like fine dust,
And the multitude of the ruthless ones like the chaff which blows away;
And it shall happen instantly, suddenly.
From the LORD of hosts you will be punished with thunder and
earthquake and loud noise,
With whirlwind and tempest and the flame of a consuming fire.
And the multitude of all the nations who wage war against Ariel,
Even all who wage war against her and her stronghold, and who
distress her,
Shall be like a dream, a vision of the night.
And it will be as when a hungry man dreams—
And behold, he is eating;
But when he awakens, his hunger is not satisfied,
Or as when a thirsty man dreams—
And behold, he is drinking,
But when he awakens, behold, he is faint,
And his thirst is not quenched.
Thus the multitude of all the nations shall be,
Who wage war against Mount Zion...
Then the Lord said, "Because this people draw near with their words
And honor Me with their lip service,
But they remove their hearts far from Me,
And their reverence for Me consists of tradition learned by rote,
Therefore behold, I will once again deal marvelously with this
people, wondrously marvelous;
And the wisdom of their wise men shall perish,
And the discernment of their discerning men shall be concealed."
Woe to those who deeply hide their plans from the LORD,
And whose deeds are done in a dark place,
And they say, "Who sees us?" or "Who knows us?"
You turn things around!
Shall the potter be considered as equal with the clay,

That what is made should say to its maker, "He did not make me";
Or what is formed say to him who formed it,
"He has no understanding"? (Is. 29:1–8, 13–16)

And so to these critics from Jerusalem, Jesus appeals to a prophecy of destruction on Jerusalem, especially on those who are reputable in a "wisdom" and a "discernment" that "consists of tradition learned by rote" (Is. 29:13–14).

If Jesus had Isaiah on His mind as He responded to the scribes, that may explain why He singled out (of many possible targets for criticism) how they treated their parents.

> Woe to the one who quarrels with his Maker—
> An earthenware vessel among the vessels of earth!
> Will the clay say to the potter, "What are you doing?"
> Or the thing you are making say, "He has no hands"?
> Woe to him who says to a father, "What are you begetting?"
> Or to a woman, "To what are you giving birth?" (Is. 8:9–10)

An offense against God is compared in Isaiah 8 to an offense against one's parents. Jesus appeals to Isaiah 29 to rebuke the scribes because, "Neglecting the commandment of God, you hold to the tradition of men" (Mk. 7:8). The offense here is not only that the scribes place their traditions on par with God's Word, but that they actually make their traditions *superior* to God's Word because they neglect the latter in order to hold to the former.

Naturally, the best illustration one can use for such a sin is an action in which one sets aside one's obligation to authority for one's own well being. Setting aside God's Word in favor of one's own word is easily comparable, especially in light of Isaiah 8:9-10, to setting aside one's obligation to one's parents in favor of one's own enjoyment of one's estate. Corrupt fundraising for the Kingdom is not, it seems, a new practice that arose with the advent of television ministries and direct mail. The Pharisees had developed a teaching which allowed a person to promise his inheritance to the religious system and thus be exempt from using it to support his aged parents. This denial of obligations to parents Jesus sees as the equivalent of the clay claiming equality with the potter or a handcraft denying that it was made (Is. 29:16).

There is something odd about Jesus' selection of Old Testament Scriptures. He quotes from the Fifth Commandment given from Mount Sinai but drops the promise attached to it. Instead He quotes from Exodus 21:17, a passage that seems off topic. What is at issue is that the scribes are encouraging those who follow them not to provide proper honor (i.e. material support, c.f Rom. 13:7; 1 Tim. 5:3, 16) for their parents. The answer has to be that, even in Jesus' move from woes on Jerusalem to His critique of Pharisaical tradition in matters of familial ethics, He does not end His hints of national judgment. What the scribes from Jerusalem are doing is not just wrong, but is even deserving of death.

> He who curses his father or his mother shall surely be put to death. (Exod. 21:17)

> If there is anyone who curses his father or his mother, he shall surely be put to death; he has cursed his father or his mother, his bloodguiltiness is upon him. (Lev. 20:9)

> He who speaks evil of father or mother is to be put to death. (Mk. 7:10b)

Now, according to the common Greek translation of the Hebrew, "speak evil" is a possible interpretation of the verb "curse," but the whole New Testament corpus tells us that there are other interpretive options Jesus could have used in Aramaic, which Mark would not have translated as "speak evil." The immediate context of Jesus' quotation indicates that He wanted to use a more generic term in order to make a specific point about how Exodus 21:17 and Leviticus 20:8 should be applied. Here is a quotation of verses Mark 7:10–12 with italics and a slightly more literal translation to point out the connections:

> For Moses said, "Honor your father and your mother;" and, "He who *speaks evil* of father or mother, let him be put to death;" but you *speak*, "If a man *speaks* to his father or his mother, 'Anything of mine you might have been helped by is Corban'" [that is to say, given to God], you no longer permit him to do anything for his father or his mother.

The scribes are speaking evil of parents by perpetuating a false doctrine that encourages their followers to speak evil of their parents. The evil they speak is "Anything of mine you might have been helped by is Corban." Thus, the entire system of economic exploitation is a corporate capital crime. Judgment is mentioned intentionally. It is at the door. Jesus drops the promise of long-life attached to the

Fifth Commandment and replaces it with a death threat.

This cryptic hint of judgment due to failure to support one's parents fits quite comfortably within a larger scheme found both throughout the Prophets and in the Gospels of judgment on economic oppressors. In this case the oppression is committed against aged parents by their children but sponsored by the scribes and done to acquire more wealth for God's representatives. We will revisit this in Mark when Jesus witnesses the widow giving all that she has into the maw of the Temple and then predicts the destruction of the Temple (Mk. 12:41ff). Indeed, Jesus makes clear that one reason for judgment coming on Jerusalem is that the scribes "devour widows' houses" (12:40).

HONORING PARENTS TODAY

By way of modern application, it is worth pointing out briefly that the Apostle Paul generalizes the Fifth Commandment to include a general responsibility for one's immediate family that includes both parents and grandparents, but others as well.

> Honor widows who are widows indeed; but if any widow has children or grandchildren, let them first learn to practice piety in regard to their own family, and to make some return to their parents; for this is acceptable in the sight of God . . . . Prescribe these things as well, so that they may be above reproach. But if anyone does not provide for his own, and especially for those of his household, he has denied the faith, and is worse than an unbeliever. (1 Tim. 5:3–4, 7–8)

It is noteworthy that these directions are given in the context, not of a list of family responsibilities, but rather in a list of *Church* responsibilities. Honoring one's father and mother now means the Church is supposed to support aged and worthy widows. One way the Church does this efficiently is by having Christian families provide for their own so that the Church is not overwhelmed by the number who need support.

Thus we see both the security and the flexibility of the Fifth Commandment. It does not limit one's obligation to one's immediate biological parents. Rather, it means one must especially provide for one's "own," including children and servants. The Bible would suggest that a Christian housekeeper for a Christian family should receive aid in times of financial crisis from that family, not necessarily from the deacon's fund of their church.

Furthermore, whether one gets support obviously depends on need. Parents who have saved for themselves do not have any right to make monetary demands on their children. We no longer live in an agrarian land-based society where one's estate consists of a piece of productive land that someone (one's heirs)must work. We can and do prepare to support ourselves in the future. Again, the application of the Fifth Commandment allows for flexibility as the Church grows in different kinds of societies with different economic systems and methods of acquiring and saving wealth.

THE POLITICS OF HOLINESS

We ought to stop a moment and consider this conflict between Jesus and the scribes as a snapshot of what had gone wrong with the Pharisees in general. The fact that they added requirements to the Law of God is nothing new here. The fact that their additional requirements actually ended up subtracting from the actual requirements that God had given in the Hebrew Scriptures is not all that surprising either. Eventually human traditions and God's Word were bound to come into conflict. But we have here a clear window into the Pharisaical mindset.

They wanted to be holier.

> For the Pharisees and all the Jews do not eat unless they carefully wash their hands, thus observing the traditions of the elders; and when they come from the market place, they do not eat unless they cleanse themselves; and there are many other things which they have received in order to observe, such as the washing of cups and pitchers and copper pots. (Mk. 7:3–4)

There are many cleanliness ordinances and cleansing rituals given in the Pentateuch. What is noticeable here is that the Pharisees and all the Jews want to be cleaner than the Law of God requires. In being concerned about eating, they were following what God said:

Hence I have said to you, "You are to possess their land, and I
Myself will give it to you to possess it, a land flowing with milk and
honey." I am the LORD your God, who has separated you from the
peoples. You are therefore to make a distinction between the clean
animal and the unclean, and between the unclean bird and the
clean; and you shall not make yourselves detestable by animal or
by bird or by anything that creeps on the ground, which I have
separated for you as unclean. Thus you are to be holy to Me, for I
the LORD am holy; and I have set you apart from the peoples to be
Mine. (Lev. 20:24–26)

You are the sons of the LORD your God . . . for you are a holy people
to the LORD your God; and the LORD has chosen you to be a
people for His own possession out of all the peoples who are
on the face of the earth. You shall not eat any detestable thing.
(Deut. 14:1a; 2–3)

The passage from Deuteronomy goes on to list clean and unclean animals, which are permitted and prohibited respectively.
These passages and others like them set up for us an understanding that God is holy and that His people both are holy and must
be holy—that is, must remain in the holy status and calling they
have been given. One way they do this is by putting only certain
things inside them.

Now, the Law does not explicitly mention every conceiveable
situation. In order to apply God's Word to new circumstances, one
must take the principle embodied in the Law and extrapolate how
it would be honored in a different state of affairs. So far, there is
nothing controversial about what the scribes were doing. No one
can do otherwise if the Bible is to have any relevance to their lives.

But the principle that the scribes seem to have fixated upon was
"holiness" and their application was to increase the required
cleansings. And if they increased the number of cleansings, it follows that they increased the number of the required separations.
This is exactly what we find in Mark, in all the other Gospels, and in Acts.

And when the scribes of the Pharisees saw that He was eating
with the sinners and tax-gatherers, they began saying to His disciples, "Why is He eating and drinking with tax-gatherers and
sinners?" (Mk. 2:16)

They led Jesus therefore from Caiaphas into the Praetorium, and it was early; and they themselves did not enter into the Praetorium in order that they might not be defiled, but might eat the Passover. (Jn. 18:28)

You yourselves know how unlawful it is for a man who is a Jew to associate with a foreigner or to visit him; and yet God has shown me that I should not call any man unholy or unclean. (Acts 10:28)

Now the apostles and the brethren who were throughout Judea heard that the Gentiles also had received the word of God. And when Peter came up to Jerusalem, those who were circumcised took issue with him, saying, "You went to uncircumcised men and ate with them." (Acts 11:1–3)

Passing over for the moment the reference from Mark's Gospel, one should notice that nowhere in the Hebrew Scriptures does the Bible say that that an Israelite could become unclean by entering the home of a Gentile. Nor is it ever considered unlawful to visit a foreigner just because he is a foreigner. Search the Scriptures and you will not find one passage forbidding a circumcised Jew from eating with an uncircumcised Gentile, and you will find many counterexamples. When Peter says it is "unlawful" for him "to associate with a foreigner" he is citing not the Law of God, but scribal traditions (Acts 10:28). Thus, when he also states that "I most certainly understand now that God is not one to show partiality, but in every nation the man who fears Him and does what is right, is welcome to Him" (Acts 10:34), he is *not* stating some new arrangement brought about by the work of Christ, but an aspect of the eternal nature of God that is plainly revealed in the Old Testament, but which the interpretive traditions of first-century Judaism had obscured and inverted. God is not the God of the Jews only but of all the nations (Rom. 3:29).

Now, if eating with the unclean (Gentiles) makes one unclean, then a person who would otherwise be clean (a Jew) but ate with Gentiles or otherwise compromised his cleanliness by, say, failing to ceremonially wash his hands, would also then be unclean. Thus, a "faithful" Jew, by the standard of scribal tradition, would have to refuse to eat not only with Gentiles but also with other Israelites who failed to maintain their purity according to these extraneous rules. Increased separation between Gentiles and Jews would mandate separation between Jews faithful to the Pharisaical code and compromised Jews who did not observe it.

This brings us to Jesus' early conflict in Mark 2 where Jesus is accused of eating with tax-gatherers and sinners. Jesus plays along with the Pharisaical game, using the dispute to assert His own authority to forgive sinners rather than arguing about the label the scribes or Pharisees were pasting on Jesus' dinner companions. After all, even if tax-gatherers were not, by definition, engaged in sin, they were often tempted to line their pockets with ill-gotten gain (cf., Lk. 3:12–13; 19:1–10). They would be all the more prone to exploit their countrymen if their countrymen regarded them as apostates simply for collecting taxes whether or not they were corrupt or honest. Likewise, human nature would dictate that, if your religious leaders regarded you as accursed by God because you didn't keep all their made-up demands, you would be all the more likely to break some of God's commands since you would probably think you were without hope anyway. Nevertheless, it may well be that many of those called "sinners" among Jesus' company were not covenant-breakers with God, but merely those who didn't adopt a Pharisaical mode of life.

Quite frankly, we see the horror of Pharisaism running wild in North American denominationalism. Constantly, the prohibition of one practice or another that is nowhere condemned in the Bible is made the basis for a new denominational identity. Tribalism is virtually paraded and boasted in as the fruit of the Protestant Reformation. Out there are all the "sinners" who don't educate their children in the correct way or who drink the wrong beverages or who don't carve up the duties of the husband and the wife in precisely the right manner. In our congregation or denomination are those who do it right and are thus superior to all others.

To cite just one example among many, one does not have to travel long in Christian circles, especially in allegedly conservative Reformed circles, to hear of a pastor's wife telling a woman that she could never be her friend because she saw her attending Sunday morning worship in a back-buttoned dress while carrying her infant child. God wants all mothers to breast feed and only wants us to befriend those who do likewise, unless they are prospective converts to true holiness—which, of course, includes and entails breast feeding.

This culture of unending schism is the antithesis of Jesus' Gospel. Against the Pharisaical game of unending "holier-than-thou" cliques, Jesus brought about one body to be known for her visible unity in love (Jn. 17:21). Thus, the Apostle Paul maintained that Christians were supposed to show hospitality to one another and not bring up differences in lifestyle (Rom. 14). We are supposed to regard everyone who confesses Jesus as Lord as possessed of God's Holy Spirit (1 Cor. 12:3). We are entreated to walk in a manner worthy of the calling with which we have been called, with all humility and gentleness, with patience, showing forbearance to one another in love, being diligent to preserve the unity of the Spirit in the bond of peace, because we are members of one body and one Spirit, just as also we were called in one hope of our calling; one Lord, one faith, one baptism, one God and Father of all who is over all and through all and in all (cf., Eph. 4:1–6). Reconciliation to God and the elimination of our real disobedience to Him cannot fail to bring about reconciliation with other men and women and the elimination of barriers based on differing practices not mandated in the Word of God.

Such an understanding would revolutionize Evangelical Christianity today. In Jesus' day it had explosive political ramifications. The Gentiles, after all, included the Romans who ruled them. Compromising these rules meant compromising with a very real enemy. Mark will show us this in stark detail when he describes the crowds siding with an insurrectionist murderer instead of their King.

THE CLEANLINESS CODE

Besides rebuking the scribes, Jesus gives an alternative interpretation of the laws of cleansing in the form of a parable and then a private interpretation for His disciples. Jesus' correction of the scribes is straight from the Law of Moses. The scribes saw in the food laws a principle that uncleanness comes from without. Jesus considered more of the data. While Mark does not give us His reasoning, he has already shown us what needs to be considered. Twice, now, Jesus has cleansed the unclean, first a leper and then a woman who had an issue of blood. In neither case was the victim unclean through touching or eating or failing to wash. In both cases the uncleanness came from within. Leprosy renders one unclean when it involves sores that are "deeper than the skin" (Lev. 13:3ff) or else are spreading. The only exception is a blemish on the head, demonstrating that some members of the body are subject to a stricter judgment.

Thus, the rules for leprosy are quite compatible with the rules for a woman's cycle. In both cases what is at issue is the revelation of what is inside. That which comes out from within us is full of sin and corruption and renders us detestable in the sight of God. Jesus is simply bringing out the meaning of the cleanliness code when He says that it is what comes from within a person that makes him unclean. The other laws should be subsumed under this principle. The reason uncleanness spreads is not because corruption and death contaminate us from "the outside." Rather, something within our own nature draws death into us. Thus, Jesus, who was without sin was unable to become unclean.

Finally, we note that Mark sees in Jesus' statement the reason why the Church gave up the dietary laws once and for all. Though they didn't get the message until Peter's vision (Acts 10), Jesus had pointed out that such laws were never meant to be permanent. Jesus himself continued to observe them, but His death was the death of such restrictions. His blood cleansed the whole world as far as the cleanliness code is concerned.

A PLACE AT THE TABLE (7:24–30)

The scribes have criticized the way the disciples "were eating their bread" (Mk. 7:2) as they have done before (Mk. 2:23ff). We might wonder if the issue of *who* Jesus allows to eat at the table with Him could be too far away. We are not allowed to wonder long.

In this case, however, it is not the scribes and/or the Pharisees who raise the issue but rather Jesus Himself. Indeed, this event need never have been associated with food at all, except that Jesus intentionally, in the presence of His disciples, insisted upon a metaphor from the family dinner table. "Let the children be satisfied first, for it is not good to take the children's bread and throw it to the dogs" (Mk. 7:27). This is a rather surprising turn of events.

By interpreting the request for an exorcism as a request for food Jesus' forces us to see real incongruity in His behavior. Why would Jesus deny table fellowship now, when in the past He has been so quick to eat with others?

But Jesus has never yet in Mark's Gospel addressed the issue of the status of Gentiles. We should know that we cannot extrapolate from how Jesus interacts with Jews who fail to live up to unbiblical holiness requirements as to how He will interact with Gentiles. The fact is that whatever He is planning to do, He has not yet at the time of this event

> made both groups into one, and broke down the barrier of the dividing wall, by abolishing in His flesh the enmity, which is the Law of commandments contained in ordinances, that in Himself He might make the two into one new man, thus establishing peace, and might reconcile them both in one body to God through the cross, by it having put to death the enmity. (Eph. 2:14b–16)

Rather, the Jew/Gentile distinction remains. The Gospels are, in a real sense, old covenant books, written about an age in which cleanliness laws were still in effect; God's special presence dwelt in one specific place, the Temple in Jerusalem; and God still had a special nation of priests. Whatever Jesus may have *intended* to do about the distinction between Jew and Gentile, the distinction still remains as appointed by God and honored by Jesus.

But we must remember that the distinction between Jew and Gentile was *never* identical to the distinction between believer and unbeliever. Needless to say, there were many Hebrews who died and were eternally lost because of unbelief. But also there were many Gentiles who, as Gentiles, believed the Gospel and inherited eternal life. Melchizedek, Jethro, Naaman, and Nebuchadnezzar are only a few. None of these men were circumcised to become Israelites, yet they believed and were saved.

Perhaps a more pertinent example can be pointed out to us by Jesus in Luke's Gospel:

> Truly I say to you, no prophet is welcome in his hometown. But I say to you in truth, there were many widows in Israel in the days of Elijah, when the sky was shut up for three years and six months, when a great famine came over all the land; and yet Elijah was sent to none of them, but only to Zarephath, in the land of Sidon, to a woman who was a widow. (4:24–26)

As it happens, Jesus' confrontation with the woman with the demon-possessed daughter occurs in the same geographical region as Elijah's encounter with the widow. In both cases a child needs deliverance—Elijah raises the widow's son (1 Kgs. 17:17–24) and Jesus exorcises the woman's daughter. And both the son and the daughter demonstrate faith by passing a test of food.

> [Elijah] called to her and said, "Please get me a little water in a jar, that I may drink." And as she was going to get it, he called to her and said, "Please bring me a piece of bread in your hand." But she said, "As the LORD your God lives, I have no bread, only a handful of flour in the bowl and a little oil in the jar; and behold, I am gathering a few sticks that I may go in and prepare for me and my son, that we may eat it and die." Then Elijah said to her, "Do not fear; go, do as you have said, but make me a little bread cake from it first, and bring it out to me, and afterward you may make one for yourself and for your son. For thus says the LORD God of Israel, 'The bowl of flour shall not be exhausted, nor shall the jar of oil be empty, until the day that the LORD sends rain on the face of the earth.'" So she went and did according to the word of Elijah, and she and he and her household ate for many days. The bowl of flour was not exhausted nor did the jar of oil become empty, according to the word of the LORD which He spoke through Elijah. (1 Kgs. 17:10b–16)

The test is clear: A Gentile must put a Hebrew prophet ahead of herself if she is to experience the deliverance of the Lord. By responding to the Syrophoenician woman with a food analogy, Jesus gave her the opportunity to pass the same test. And by God's grace and by a true and living faith she passed with flying colors, attaining salvation for her daughter.

TWO-STAGE HEARING & SPEAKING (7:31–37)

Jesus moves on to the same region in which earlier He had cast out the legion of demons and driven them into the herd of swine. In that case He conquered the army with a mere word. We are reminded of this by the exorcism He had just performed since He did so at a distance without even seeing the victim.

Yet suddenly Jesus seems to be expending more effort. The request is quite simple; they want Jesus to lay His hands on a deaf man who cannot speak clearly. But Jesus does something more elaborate. Why?

What we seem to have here are two stages in the process. First Jesus touches the problem parts. Then He sighs and commands. Let us consider Jesus' actions in the order they are listed.

When Jesus pokes His finger into the man's ear, we are reminded of the Old Testament precedent of an ear being pierced. Jesus' finger represents an awl:

> If you buy a Hebrew slave, he shall serve for six years; but on the seventh he shall go out as a free man without payment. If he comes alone, he shall go out alone; if he is the husband of a wife, then his wife shall go out with him. If his master gives him a wife, and she bears him sons or daughters, the wife and her children shall belong to her master, and he shall go out alone. But if the slave plainly says, "I love my master, my wife and my children; I will not go out as a free man," then his master shall bring him to God, then he shall bring him to the door of the doorpost. And his master shall pierce his ear with an awl; and he shall serve him permanently. (Exod. 21:2–6)

Jesus could have healed the man without poking His ear, but this sign gives watchers something to think about. Ultimately Israel's time under masters is coming to an end. Now is the time to have one's ear circumcised or else be driven out of God's household. The pierced ear means adoption into God's household as a son. We see this in Galatians where Paul stresses that the Spirit was received by "hearing with faith" (3:2) and goes on to show how all history has moved Israel and the whole human race from the tutelage of masters who treated them as slaves to the age of free adoption and inheritance as sons:

> Now I say, as long as the heir is a child, he does not differ at all from a slave although he is owner of everything, but he is under guardians and managers until the date set by the father. So also we, while we were children, were held in bondage under the elemental things of the world. But when the fullness of the time came, God sent forth His Son, born of a woman, born under the Law, in order that He might redeem those who were under the Law, that we might receive the adoption as sons. And because you are sons, God has sent forth the Spirit of His Son into our hearts, crying,

"Abba! Father!" Therefore you are no longer a slave, but a son; and if a son, then an heir through God. (Gal. 4:1–7)

So much for the finger; what about the saliva anointing the tongue? We have already mentioned that the Law of Moses showed that uncleanness flowed from within. Jesus seems to demonstrate rather vividly that from his inward parts flow streams of living water (cf., Jn. 7:38). Instead of being unclean, Jesus brings cleansing.

Yet all of these things are not enough. Jesus must do yet another thing in order to restore the man. He must breathe a sigh and look up to heaven saying, "Be opened." Taking a cue from John 20:22, it is probable that Jesus in invoking the Holy Spirit by His sigh.

But why this second act after touching the ears and tongue? Our answer will become clear when we reach the next healing miracle, the giving of sight to the blind man. In the meantime, our cycle comes to an end with the Gospel being spread (over Jesus' objections) in the story of the healing of the deaf mute. After Jesus has enabled a man to hear and speak, we find the people of the region *hearing* of what happened and *saying* that Jesus does all things well. Jesus is restoring the world to be able to hear the Gospel and speak to God's glory.

MORE SHEEP FOR THE SHEPHERD (8:1–9)

After the raising of the daughter of the Synagogue ruler, Jesus fed five thousand Israelites. Now, having cast a demon out of the daughter of a Syrophoenecian woman, Jesus feeds four thousand in the region of the Decapolis, predominately Gentile territory. Strangely, the disciples seem unable to imagine that Jesus can provide for this number, even though he already fed a greater number. Here again we find Jesus blessing and breaking bread in eucharistic fashion this time, significantly, feeding Gentiles. The numbers correlate with such guests. Four thousand is a multiple of the number of the corners of the earth and seven is a tenth of the number of the nations (Gen. 10 gives us a table of nations which adds up to seventy).

Remember that for those participating in this feast, the miraculous feeding would be more than merely an attesting sign that God was at work in Jesus. It would have the much more concrete force of showing that God was now fulfilling His great promises to Israel—and through Israel, to the nations—through Jesus.

> And the LORD of hosts will prepare a lavish banquet for all peoples
> on this mountain;
> A banquet of aged wine, choice pieces with marrow,
> And refined, aged wine.
> And on this mountain He will swallow up the covering which is
> over all peoples,
> Even the veil which is stretched over all nations.
> He will swallow up death for all time,
> And the Lord GOD will wipe tears away from all faces,
> And He will remove the reproach of His people from all the earth;
> For the LORD has spoken.
> And it will be said in that day, "Behold, this is our God for whom
> we have waited that He might save us.
> This is the LORD for whom we have waited;
> Let us rejoice and be glad in His salvation." (Is. 25:6–9)

Granted, Jesus is not yet serving wine, but His meal in the Decapolis could not fail to remind those who were literate in the Scriptures of the great promises that God had made.

THE LESSON OF THE LOAVES (8:10–21)

Yet the Pharisees do not understand. They come to Jesus and ask for a sign, as if His mission has not been exploding with more miraculous effects than a George Lucas Film! Jesus simply refuses their request and leaves them, after condemning the entire generation of which He considered them representatives.

It should be pointed out here that the next miracle will be the healing of a blind man (8:22ff). The Pharisees cannot see and represent an unseeing generation. Jesus must restore Israel's sight. The miracle before this was the healing of a deaf mute (Mk. 7:31ff). Jesus' conflict with the scribes before that healing incident had involved them honoring God with their lips while their hearts were far from Him (Mk. 7:6) and their "speaking evil" (7:10).

Of course, the first man was not only dumb but also deaf. Yet hearing too is involved in Jesus' conflict with the scribes. His antidote to the scribal error is for people to "listen . . . and understand" (7:14). When the disciples question Him privately, He immediately asks, "Are you so lacking in understanding also" (7:18). Israel needs opened ears and opened hearts.

Chapter 7: false teaching and inability to listen/understand—deaf-mute healed

Chapter 8: demand to see a sign—blind man healed

Perhaps this association between spiritual defect and physical defect explains why Mark records identical responses to one and the other. Jesus utters a deep sigh while healing the deaf-mute (Mk. 7:34). He also sighs deeply when confronted by the Pharisees (Mk 8:12).

THE LEAVEN OF THE PHARISEES & HEROD

What exactly was Jesus trying to warn the disciples about? Instead of contrasting Herod and the Pharisees, I think it would be more accurate to expect that Jesus thought they had something in common, no matter how opposed they were to one another. They certainly readily united in their opposition to Jesus Himself (Mk. 3:6; 12:13).

Given Jesus' conflict with Peter and the other disciples, we will find, I think, that for all their opposition, the Pharisees and Herod had an agreement about the fundamental nature of the Kingdom. If Herod did not believe in the Kingdom, then perhaps we should say that they were agreed on the fundamental nature of authority. Jesus will be endeavoring to teach His disciples a different kind of authority which entails that they need to change their expectations about the Kingdom as well as the King.

THE DISCIPLES' EYES, EARS, & HEARTS

But the Pharisees are not the only problem. The disciples do not get it, either. Twice now a voyage has shown their hearts to be hardened so that they are unable to perceive or understand that Jesus is trustworthy and will take care of them. This time no storm is needed to demonstrate their hardness of heart. Rather, a mere parable from Jesus causes them to discuss their lack of bread as if God had not proven to be more than sufficient. Jesus' rebuke is worded quite appropriately. The disciples take a parable about leavened bread as if the statement was concerning real bread. Jesus responds by reminding them of two miracles involving real bread, which were meant to be interpreted as parables (see above).

Indeed, Jesus once again quotes a prophet about Israel's inability to perceive, just as He did when explaining to the disciples why He was speaking to the people in parables (Mk. 4:12). The difference, of course, is that before Jesus was telling the disciples that they were going to be privileged with the revelation that others would miss. Now He is telling them that despite clear teaching they themselves are no different than the others.

The other difference that must be noted is that, though Jesus is again citing a Hebrew prophet regarding an inability to see or hear, this time it is *not* Isaiah 6 that He is quoting. Rather He appeals to Jeremiah 5:21—a passage that refers to Israel's inability to understand God's power over the sea and over the weather. Even though, on this third voyage-incident, there is no storm, the theme of God's power over the sea remains present. The sea consistently reveals the hardness of the disciples' hearts.

THE TWO-STAGE ENLIGHTENMENT (8:22–26)

Having established that the disciples, as is the case of their generation in general, can neither hear nor see, Mark tells us of a miracle that complements the last one. Having cured a deaf-mute, Jesus will now restore sight to a blind man. If we saw hints of two stages in the last healing, here it is explicit: Jesus makes two attempts to restore the man's sight, and only the second one gives clear vision.

What are we to make of this?

Jesus has established that His miracles are parables. Any doubts about that should be dispelled by the way He appeals to the numbers involved in His miraculous meals. In this case, then, Jesus is trying to show the disciples something about themselves. Earlier, in explaining His use of parables, Jesus had promised that they could see and hear the mysteries of the Kingdom. Yet He has also told them they are blind. Because of Jesus' work, the disciples see, yet they don't see clearly. That will take more work.

THE WAY OF THE CROSS & THE CHRIST (8:27–9:1)

No sooner has Jesus healed the blind man than the point of the way He performed the miracle is amply demonstrated. Peter recognizes that Jesus is the Christ, the promised King of Israel who will deliver Israel from her enemies. But though Peter sees that Jesus is the Christ, neither he nor his comrades understands what that means. They do not see clearly yet.

Jesus tells them that He is to be crucified. He is speaking what the disciples can only consider blasphemous nonsense. Christ crucified is a stumbling block to them. It is unthinkable that God's promised king would be defeated and publicly humiliated by pagan soldiers and a compromised priesthood. It makes no sense. Peter takes it upon himself to rebuke Jesus.

Jesus is not amused. He has defeated Satan in the wilderness, but now Satan is back, using Peter to present him with the powerful temptation to evade the cross. Once again, despite the Devil's use of his own disciples, Jesus overcomes.

Up until now, Jesus has been teaching publicly in parables and then explaining things privately to His disciples. Now that practice is reversed. First, Jesus gives His disciples private teaching, then He speaks public riddles:

> "If anyone wishes to come after Me, let him deny himself, and take up his cross, and follow Me. For whoever wishes to save his life shall lose it; but whoever loses his life for My sake and the gospel's shall save it. For what does it profit a man to gain the whole world, and forfeit his soul? For what shall a man give in exchange for his soul? For whoever is ashamed of Me and My words in this adulterous and sinful generation, the Son of Man will also be ashamed of him when He comes in the glory of His Father with the holy angels." And He was saying to them, "Truly I say to you, there are some of those who are standing here who shall not taste death until they see the kingdom of God after it has come with power."

We have been taught to understand what taking up one's cross means, but to that original multitude Jesus' words must have been entirely enigmatic. They had no idea that Jesus had just told His disciples that He was going to be crucified. Paradoxical statements about losing one's life and saving it (made all the more hard to untangle when one realizes that "life" and "soul" are the same word in the Greek) coupled with uninterpreted analogies involving horrific methods of execution must have left everyone scratching their heads.

The final comment by Jesus has often left modern readers scratching their heads. Who was going to live long enough to see the Kingdom come with power? The common view is that this refers to Peter, James, and John on the Mount of Transfiguration. It is more likely, however, that Jesus is referring to the eschatological expectation which framed Jesus' ministry from the beginning. John promised that Jesus would baptize with the Holy Spirit. Pentecost is the reference here, at least. Jesus has also alluded, through Isaiah 6 and 29 (Mk. 4:12; 7:6–7), to the destruction of Jerusalem that will occur in about forty years. One or both of these events is probably what Jesus is referring to by the coming of the Kingdom.

Mark 9:2–11:52

Calling & Cross

Jesus has now told the disciples about the future, His future as Christ. From here to Jerusalem, we will see Jesus trying to get His message across, but the disciples resisting it or simply misunderstanding it.

MOUNTAIN TOP TO FOOT (9:2–29)

When Jesus called the Twelve (Mk. 3:13ff), the first three are especially singled out by new names. Andrew, though technically called before James and John, is no longer listed with his brother. Peter, James, and John are called again up a new mountain for a special revelation. Indeed, though Simon's name change was announced at the calling of the Twelve, Mark applies it only now. From the time of his confession of Jesus as the Christ, Mark consistently refers to the disciple as Peter, the only exception being to quote Jesus' addressing him as Simon when he is asleep in the garden of Gethsemane. Simon's name has now changed to Peter.

The only time Mark referred to Simon as Peter before this point is the exception that proves the rule. Then Jesus selected him and James and John to witness the only resurrection recorded in Mark, other than Jesus' own (Mk. 5:37). That revelation of the power of the new creation typified this one on the Mountain—in both cases only shown to the three.

SPIRIT BAPTISM

Beyond its echoes of the calling of the Twelve and the raising of Jairus' daughter, the story of the Transfiguration reminds us of Jesus' baptism. Mark has told us the Spirit is a dove. Here he does not mention the identity of the cloud that enveloped Jesus and the three, but he does not need to. God said through Haggai that the cloud within the Tabernacle was His Spirit (Hag. 2:5). The Spirit came upon Jesus in a humble way at His baptism. Now Jesus is given the fullness of the promise of His baptism, though only temporarily. The presence of Moses, Peter's mention of Tabernacles, the presence of Elijah who was taken up in a fiery chariot while the Spirit fell upon his successor in great power all remind us of the Spirit.

The Transfiguration was a temporary preview of the nature of the resurrection:

> But someone will say, "How are the dead raised? And with what kind of body do they come?" You fool! That which you sow does not come to life unless it dies; and that which you sow, you do not sow the body which is to be, but a bare grain, perhaps of wheat or of something else. But God gives it a body just as He wished, and to each of the seeds a body of its own. All flesh is not the same flesh, but there is one flesh of men, and another flesh of beasts, and another flesh of birds, and another of fish. There are also heavenly bodies and earthly bodies, but the glory of the heavenly is one, and the glory of the earthly is another. There is one glory of the sun, and another glory of the moon, and another glory of the stars; for star differs from star in glory. So also is the resurrection of the dead. It is sown a perishable body, it is raised an imperishable body; it is sown in dishonor, it is raised in glory; it is sown in weakness, it is raised in power; it is sown a natural body, *it is raised a spiritual body*. If there is a natural body, *there is also a spiritual body*. So also it is written, "The first man, Adam, became a living soul." The last Adam became a life-giving spirit. However, the spiritual is not first, but the natural; then the spiritual. The first man is from the earth, earthy; the second man is from heaven. As is the earthy, so also are those who are earthy; and as is the heavenly, so also are those who are heavenly. And just as we have borne the image of the earthy, we shall also bear the image of the heavenly. Now I say this, brethren, that flesh and blood cannot inherit the kingdom of God; nor does the perishable inherit the imperishable. Behold, I tell you a mystery; we shall not all sleep, but we shall all be changed, in a moment, in the twinkling of an eye, at the last trumpet; for the trumpet will sound, and the dead will be raised imperishable, and we shall be changed. For this perishable must put on the imperishable, and this mortal must put on immortality. (1 Cor. 15:35–53; emphasis added)

The Spirit came upon Jesus at His baptism, but now He has a Spiritual body. In the twinkling of an eye, Jesus has a perishable body of flesh, and blood has put on the imperishable.

There are many other clues that what is happening now is a fulfillment of the beginning of Jesus' ministry. John the Baptist dressed like Elijah (Mk. 1:6; 2 Kgs. 1:8) and now Elijah appears. The Father's voice is heard again declaring Jesus to be His Son (Mk. 1:11; 9:7). Three of the original four disciples are present. Mark is showing that Jesus has reached a new stage. His mission is beginning again. The call on him in baptism is now being fulfilled.

GLORIFIED HUMANITY

Before we go any further, I need to warn readers of a common error regarding the Transfiguration. The Transfiguration did *not* reveal Jesus' deity. More than one preacher has claimed from the pulpit that Jesus was "God in disguise" until the mask was removed during the Transfiguration. But Jesus never disguised God; He revealed Him. The popular Christmas carol has it exactly backwards. Godhead was never "veiled in flesh," but rather *manifested* in flesh. When Jesus said that, "He who has seen Me has seen the Father" (Jn. 14:9), He was speaking not to Peter, James, or John, but to Phillip who never witnessed the Transfiguration.

The Transfiguration was not a revelation of deity, but rather a revelation of true humanity. God created human beings to reflect His glory. Thus, Moses' face shone after he beheld the glory of God (Exod. 33:18; 34:8, 29–35). Thus, Stephen's face will become like that of an angel when the heavens open above the Sanhedrin and Stephen sees Jesus at the right hand of God (Acts 7). We were made to glow; sin has dimmed us.

Any doubt about this should be put to rest by Peter's sacrilege. He suggests that Jesus and Moses and Elijah all be given equal honor in three tabernacles. All three were revealed in glory. It was the voice of the Father that revealed Jesus' uniqueness from the other two.

THE RESURRECTION

While it is obvious that Peter erred in wanting to give equal honor to the three, there may be another mistake involved in his suggestion, "Rabbi, it is good for us to be here" (Mk. 9:5). Luke makes plain that Peter said this when Moses and Elijah were about to leave (Lk. 9:33). If Peter wanted to remain on the mountain, then he has incorrectly assumed that because Jesus now appears to him in glory, such glory may be given to him without cost. Jesus knows it comes with a price. It is the glory He will have at His resurrection. But now He must go down the mountain and leave the glory behind.

On the way down, Jesus forbids His disciples to tell what they have seen until after His resurrection. We might tend to be overly harsh on Peter, James, and John for not immediately understanding what Jesus was talking about. But remember that Jesus had just strongly rebuked the disciples for taking Him literally when He meant something figuratively—namely leaven (Mk. 8:14–21). Furthermore, one major text in the Hebrew Scriptures, which mentions the resurrection, is a metaphorical passage (Ezek. 37).

Jesus does not rebuke them for their inability to understand him, but rather directs them to think on the implications of His relationship to John the Baptist and John's to Elijah. Ahab never captured Elijah and Elijah marched freely over the path through the parted Jordan to be assumed into heaven aboard a fiery chariot. Elijah received his glory for "free."

But John the Baptist had received no visible glory at all, grotesquely beheaded on the basis of a young girl's pleasing dance. God's servants are treading a new path in these later times. Jesus will only inherit His glory at His resurrection. Daniel's prophecy of persecution for the saints Jesus applies directly and uniquely to Himself: "[H]ow is it written of the Son of Man that He should suffer many things and be treated with contempt?" (Mk. 9:12; Dan. 9:25)

UNBELIEVING GENERATION

When Jesus inveighs against this "unbelieving generation," we are reminded of Psalm 95:10.[1]

[1] "The reaction of Jesus is half a quotation from Psalm 95:10 . . ." R. Alan Cole, *Mark* (Grand Rapids, Michigan: Eerdmans, 1989), 215.

For forty years I loathed that generation,
And said they are a people who err in their heart,
And they do not know My ways.

Here is another generation who, though located in the Promised Land, are nevertheless headed for a death in the wilderness if they do not repent. Within forty years Rome will invade and destroy that unbelieving generation.

Psalm 95 mentions the incident in the wilderness at Massah and Meribah, but the sequence reminds us also of what happened at Mount Sinai. Like Jesus, Moses went up into the cloud and then returned to the people waiting at the bottom of the mountain. There he found that they had been faithless (Exod. 32:1ff). Jesus likewise finds a father lacking in faith and His disciples lacking in prayer.

Why couldn't the disciples cast out the demon? Jesus' explanation is somewhat puzzling; the disciples had been able to cast out demons before since Jesus had given them the authority to do so. Why should some demons be under such authority while others require additional prayer?

Within this part of Mark's Gospel, Jesus' casual observation does seem to be an exhortation to self-sacrificial service. Consider what happens before and after this passage:

Suffering Predicted

Mark 8:31	Mark 9:9–13	Mark 9:30–31
"Son of Man must suffer...and be killed, and after three days rise again..."	"the Son of Man should rise from the dead...the Son of Man...should suffer..."	"The Son of Man is to be delivered into the hands of men...and after He has been killed, He will rise three days later."

Disciples Unbelieving

Mark 8:32	Mark 9:33	Mark 9:33
Peter rebukes Jesus	"What were you discussing with them?"	"What were you discussing on the way?"

Jesus' Exhortation

Mark 8:33–9:1	Mark 9:29	Mark 9:35ff
Take up cross	Demon requires prayer	Be like a child

It seems that Jesus is trying to teach His disciples the way of the cross. He has decided no longer to allow them to have automatically the powers He originally gave them. Jesus tells them they could have overcome the demon if they had prayed. Later He will beg the disciples to "keep watching and praying that you may not come into temptation" (Mk. 14:38). Jesus, though He is very God of very God, has not hesitated to pray often and long. The disciples, if Peter is representative, will be full of overconfident zeal, sure that they can overcome any trial. They will not learn the lesson of the demon that only comes out by prayer.

Nor do they seem to really learn the lesson of the father who realizes his incapacity to trust as he ought. "I do believe; help my unbelief" (Mk. 9:24), is a cry that the disciples should have emulated.

PRIVATE TEACHING & DEAF EARS (9:30–50)

Jesus teaches His disciples again that He must suffer and die and rise again. This time Peter knows better than to rebuke him, but the disciples are quite obviously refusing to listen to Jesus' message. They begin an argument about who will be the greatest once Jesus has assumed the throne. Since this is the second time that Jesus' message that He must die is met with unbelief, perhaps we should compare the two incidents.[2]

When Jesus first began teaching the fate of the Son of Man, His discourse began with a question: "Who do people say that I am?" (Mk. 8:27). So it is now. Jesus asks what the disciples have been discussing. Peter affirms Jesus as God's anointed King and Jesus responds by teaching that this Davidic king is not going to triumph in the same way as His forefather has done before him. The Christ is commissioned to walk the way of the cross. Indeed, Jesus questioned His disciples while they were "on the way" (Mk. 8:27) and He later wants to know what they were discussing "on the way"—and Mark repeats the phrase twice to make sure we do not miss it (Mk. 9:33–34). Jesus like Solomon in the book of Proverbs is trying to teach His sons about kingly wisdom and the way of the Lord.[3]

---

[2] Following Austin Farrer, *A Study in Saint Mark* (New York, Oxford Univ. Press, 1952) 112, 113.

[3] Again, as mentioned in the first chapter, I owe these observations about wisdom in Mark's gospel to Jeff Meyers, especially his lectures on Mark for the 1997 Biblical Horizons' conference. They are available from Biblical Horizons, P. O. Box 1096, Niceville, FL 32588.

In this second incident, we find the disciples unable to understand the way of the cross, arguing for who will be first in Jesus' royal entourage. Jesus has to explain that the servant cannot be greater than the master. If the King himself is to be crucified, the King's men cannot expect to inherit wealth and power through self-exaltation. The paradoxical wisdom of the way of the Lord is that the King's servants who humble themselves as children are the one's that may be His ambassadors.

Indeed we see Mark's irony in that he never quoted the nature of the disciples' authority when Jesus sent them out (Mk. 6:7–11). But now that Jesus has a child on His lap, He quotes to them the same words that He said to them as His ambassadors, as we can deduce by comparing the sending of the Twelve in the Gospel of Matthew.

> And taking a child, He set him before them, and taking him in His arms, He said to them, "Whoever receives one child like this in My name receives Me; and whoever receives Me does not receive Me, but Him who sent Me." (Mk. 9:36–37)

> These twelve Jesus sent out after instructing them, saying … "He who receives you receives Me, and he who receives Me receives Him who sent Me. He who receives a prophet in the name of a prophet shall receive a prophet's reward; and he who receives a righteous man in the name of a righteous man shall receive a righteous man's reward. And whoever in the name of a disciple gives to one of these little ones even a cup of cold water to drink, truly I say to you he shall not lose his reward." (Mt. 10:5a, 40–42)

Thus, the authority of a minister as emissary of Jesus and God is not explicitly given to Jesus' disciples but to children. Arguing about precedence has no place.

After Jesus asked the disciples who the people said He was, Peter became zealous for Jesus' royal status and rebuked Him for claiming He was going to be killed. In our second incident it is John who shows zeal—zeal, this time, against someone who has acted without a proper commission to cast out demons in Jesus' name. But a King who is determined to go the way of the cross does not need a company of men zealous to maintain a monopoly on power.

Jesus goes on to exhort them to receive the little ones in His name and then to be willing to give up anything that they might enter the Kingdom. Gehenna was a valley outside Jerusalem notorious as a place once given over to human sacrifices (2 Chr. 28:3; 33:6; Jer. 7:31; 32:35). It would correspond to an unclean place outside the camp in the days of the Tabernacle in the wilderness. In those days, Aaron and his sons were consecrated as priests by a ceremony which included anointing the right thumb, the right big toe, and the ear with blood (Lev. 8:22–24), representing the hand, foot, and head, respectively. Thus, Jesus names these three things as those that must be sacrificed for the sake of the Kingdom, though He represents the head by an eye rather than an ear. Jesus is calling them to complete devotion to their new callings, just as the Aaronic priests were called to devotion in their ordination rite.

This leads us to an understanding of what is meant by salt. Contrary to popular belief in modern New Testament teaching, the ancients were well used to salt as a flavor that makes food taste better. "Can something tasteless be eaten without salt, or is there any taste in the white of an egg?" (Job 6:6). What is more, God revealed to the Israelites that He liked grain offerings better with salt. "Every grain offering of yours, moreover, you shall season with salt, so that the salt of the covenant of your God shall not be lacking from your grain offering; with all your offerings you shall offer salt" (Lev. 2:13). Food going up as smoke from burning on the altar hardly needs to be preserved! But if God can be said to consume the sacrifices, then the salt would be seasoning for His meal.

In fact, it was the special privilege of the priests, as the ones appointed to put food on God's table, that they would season God's offerings. Thus, God tells Aaron

> All the offerings of the holy gifts, which the sons of Israel offer to the LORD, I have given to you and your sons and your daughters with you, as a perpetual allotment. It is an everlasting covenant of salt before the LORD to you and your descendants with you. (Num. 18:19)

When Abijah rebukes the Northern Kingdom for separating themselves from the Temple worship at Jerusalem, he sums it up by asking rhetorically, "Do you not know that the LORD God of Israel gave the rule over Israel forever to David and his sons by a covenant of salt?" (2 Chr. 13:5)

In the New Covenant we are to offer up our bodies as living sacrifices. Jesus is warning His disciples not to lose their flavor. If they will receive the little ones and be humble themselves, they will remain salty. Furthermore, they will have peace with one another, instead of arguing about who is the greatest.

PUBLIC TEACHING: MARRIAGE, CHILDREN, & WEALTH (10:1–31)

Leaving Peter's home in Capernaum, the prototype church where Jesus gave His disciples private teaching, Jesus now moves to a public forum. The successor of Moses and Elijah stations Himself in the region where Elijah was taken up into heaven and Moses gave his last sermon before ascending Mount Nebo to his death. His sermon comes to us in the Bible as the book of Deuteronomy, and that is exactly the text that Jesus will be discussing.

MARRIAGE

John the Baptist was also located in the region of the Jordan, and he was killed because he criticized Herod for taking his brother's wife. When we are told that the Pharisees were "testing" Jesus (10:2), we begin to suspect that they would like nothing more then for Jesus to run afoul of Herod for criticizing his matrimonial practices.

Jesus, having come from an interview with Moses in a glory-cloud now stands where Moses last preached and defends Moses

---

[4] The popular idea that Deuteronomy 24:1ff does not acknowledge any such legal right but rather places controls on a sinful practice is ingenious grammatically but nevertheless impossible to sustain. A practice which a person is permitted to do unless he commits certain wrongs so that he loses this permission (Deut. 22:19, 29) is indistinguishable from a legal right that is taken away as a penalty for some actions. The fact that God prohibited divorce in some cases indicates that He could have stopped it in all cases. To use the grammar of Deuteronomy 24:1 to say that a right to divorce is never actually granted is a striking example of legal rationalization.

Example: If a nineteenth-century U.S. law stated, "When a settler wants to kill a Native American, he must file a write of notice with the local Cavalry commander before he does so," and prescribed no penalty for such an act, wouldn't it be correct to say that the Federal from his misinterpreters. The Pharisees want male-oriented no-fault divorce and are justifying themselves by Moses, who acknowledges a husband's right to divorce his wife,[4] mandating he give her a "book of divorce" and prohibiting him from remarrying her if she marries and divorces another man. The question is whether God meant for the husband to decide what constitutes the "indecency in her" that allows him to divorce her (Deut. 24:1). Basically, the Pharisaical position (at least that of the Pharisees confronting Jesus in this incident) is that Moses allows a husband to divorce his wife for any reason he wants to, as long as he fills out the requisite paperwork.

Jesus replies that it is only due to sin that divorce was ever permitted. The original plan was that husband and wives live in love forever. They were joined together by God. After sin came, marriages began to be targeted by unfaithfulness, and the law was given to Moses to account for the new situation. Hardness of hearts means that a wife might be unfaithful and a husband have to use his recourse to Deuteronomy 24:1ff.

As if Jesus was speaking in parables, His disciples come to speak to Him privately (Mk. 10:10ff). Jesus then explicitly states that those throwing away their wives and getting remarried are guilty of adultery. If all we had to guide us was Mark, we might think here that Jesus forever condemned divorce for any reason. However, Mark knows that he is not our only guide and expects us to know from the Old Testament and from Deuteronomic text itself, that there are exceptions to the general rule. In any case,

---

government's laws gave settlers the right to kill Native Americans? Wouldn't any argument that the Federal government never said it was legal to kill Native Americans be considered an insufficient reply? And if another law said that a settler who steals a horse is no longer permitted to kill a Native American, wouldn't that be all the more evidence that killing Native Americans was a legal right granted by the U.S. government?

Furthermore, Deuteronomy 24:1ff is a law that manifests the character of God: "And I saw that for all the adulteries of faithless Israel, I had sent her away and given her a writ of divorce, yet her treacherous sister Judah did not fear; but she went and was a harlot also" (Jer. 3:8). "Thus says the LORD, 'Where is the certificate of divorce, by which I have sent your mother away? Or to whom of My creditors did I sell you? Behold, you were sold for your iniquities, and for your transgressions your mother was sent away" (Is. 50:1). How

Matthew tells us that Jesus mentioned an exception—immorality (5:32).

CHILDREN

Having protected women from easy divorce, Mark now shows us Jesus' regard for children. Here his public teaching at the Jordan reiterates His private teaching in Capernaum (Mk. 9:36). The disciples attempt to keep children away from Jesus, but Jesus responds in indignation, insisting that the Kingdom belongs to those who are childlike.

Realizing that Mark is giving us a reiteration of what Jesus said in private to the disciples gives us a new perspective on the entire controversy regarding divorce. As leaders and pastors, the scribes and Pharisees were found by Jesus to be wanting. They "devour widows' houses" (Mk. 12:40), a sin not too far from promoting easy divorce for men. Jesus wants His disciples to be better pastors—to show concern for widows and orphans, for women and children.

WEALTH

Jesus' last bit of private teaching was about casting away hand, foot, or eye in order to enter life. Now a rich and righteous man comes before Him and asks what he must do to inherit eternal life. Jesus asks him if he is faithfully keeping covenant with God and the youth replies that he has. There is no reason in the world to insist that the young man was deceiving himself or even imagined his words to possibly mean that he had never sinned. The Law of God was given for sinners as the way of living by faith. Everything about

---

can anyone dare say that God would never approve of divorce? Presumably he approves of his own. Would not a godly man possibly be put in a similar situation and need to invoke Deuteronomy 24:1ff?

Finally, Deuteronomy 24:1ff is commonly disparaged as a "no-fault" allowance because it is believed that anything that would permit a husband to divorce his wife would entail a mandatory death penalty. But the death penalties for adultery and other such crimes were maximal, not mandatory. See James B. Jordan's *The Law of the Covenant: An Exposition of Exodus 21–23* (Tyler: ICE, 1985) 148, 149.

Jesus indicates that He approved of the young man's response to His question.

But Israel is under judgment, and all Israelites need to flee the wrath to come. This young man needs to trade what he has for a place in Jesus' company. He finds that he can't do it. His faith and faithfulness reach an end. He cannot trust Jesus enough to actually believe that he should give up his wealth to gain greater riches.

Not everyone is called to give up all their wealth and give it to the poor, just as not everyone is called to build a giant three-story boat and load it up with pairs of animals. But like the impending flood, Jesus saw judgment coming and He was giving the young man a ready way of escaping it. In general, it is permissible for godly men to earn a living and even acquire wealth without devoting time and money to building a great big boat. But if Noah had loved his life-style too much to build the Ark, his permissible life-style would have been revealed to be unlawful idolatry. Jesus never quoted the first four commandments to the rich young man. The reason is not hard to see. Whether or not he had become an idolater would be revealed by his response to God's call. Sometimes wealth is a fortress from God. Sometimes it is a trap of Satan. And sometimes it turns from one to the other.

The disciples are astonished that the rich enter the kingdom only with difficulty (Mk. 10:24). As N. T. Wright puts it,

> Some Jews assumed, perhaps on the basis of a facile reading of Deuteronomy and certain psalms, that wealth was a sign of YHWH's favor. It signaled, apparently, that one was already in receipt of covenant blessings. This explains the disciples' great surprise ("they were exceedingly astonished," Mk. 10.25) at being told that rich people would have difficulty inheriting the kingdom. They *assumed* that the rich were going to be part of the kingdom; the question for them was, who else? But Jesus was saying that the rich were not only not automatically within the covenant, but very likely outside it. This completely overturned the disciples' worldview; but it was not a new thing in Jesus' preaching. There were ... other warnings to the rich. When "the age to come" finally arrived, possessions and property would have nothing whatever to do with membership.[5]

[5] N.T. Wright, *Jesus & the Victory of God* (Minneapolis: Fortress Press, 1996) 303–304.

The disciples, Jesus does not hesitate to say, have chose the winning team. Everything they gave up to join with Him will be replaced and more besides. Israel is facing imminent judgment so that "many first will be last; and the last first" (Mk. 10:31).

GOD'S SOVEREIGNTY & MAN'S (10:32–45)

The disciples still don't get it. Once again Jesus tries to explain to them the way of the cross while they are "on the way" to Jerusalem (Mk. 10:32; c. f. 8:27; 9:33–34).[6] Once again we have a three-stage incident:

Suffering Predicted	10:32–34— "Son of man will be delivered up…"
Disciples Unbelieving	10:35–40—James & John ask to be preeminent, enthroned with Jesus.
Jesus' Exhortation	10:41–45— "And calling them to himself…"

Jesus, as we will see, is recognized as the divine King in His crucifixion. When James and John ask to be enthroned with Him, "one on Your right, and one on Your left" (10:37), they are undoubtedly thinking that this will happen once they arrive at Jerusalem. And they are right. God's King does assume His throne in Jerusalem. Indeed, had they remained with Jesus in His sufferings, they may have won the honor of being raised up on either side of Him. But the honor went to two insurgents.

Jesus calls the disciples together to try to heal the rift between them and teach them about true sovereignty. The disciples, like the Pharisees, have received their ideas about rule and power from the Gentiles. They affirm that God is a great King but then get their ideas about kingliness from Caesar and Herod. Even though they hate those rulers, they have received their fundamental assumptions about what it means to rule from them. Jesus sets before

---

[6] The NASB says "on the road" this time, but the Greek is identical.

them the true nature of the Son of Man and thus the true character of God. "The Son of Man did not come to be served, but to
serve and to give His live as a ransom for many" (Mk. 10:45).

CASTING ASIDE TO FOLLOW (10:46–52)

Jesus has exorcised a boy who could neither hear nor speak. Now
He finishes with a fully-restored head by healing a blind man. Earlier Mark told us that the rich man ran up to Jesus. Obviously a
blind man cannot run anywhere. But he can shout and scream
until he is heard. Jesus responds to his name by calling him. It is
rather interesting that Mark tells us that blind Bartimaeus cast
aside his cloak to go to Jesus (10:50), but he never tells us that he
retrieved it. Furthermore, Jesus allows him to go wherever he wills,
yet he insists on following Jesus (10:52).

Bartimaeus is the opposite of the rich man. Bartimaeus is poor,
yet he willingly parts with what he does have to follow Jesus. He
shows why it is easier for the poor to enter the Kingdom, for
Baritmaeus has very little to lose and his sight to gain.

In reality, of course, none of us have anything to lose and a great
deal to gain, but our eyes prevent us from seeing that.

Calling & Confrontation

W hen King Solomon assumed the throne, David devised two signs by which he would claim his kingdom:

> Take with you the servants of your lord, and have my son Solomon ride on my own mule, and bring him down to Gihon. And let Zadok the priest and Nathan the prophet anoint him there as king over Israel, and blow the trumpet and say, "Long live King Solomon!" Then you shall come up after him, and he shall come and sit on my throne and be king in my place; for I have appointed him to be ruler over Israel and Judah. (1 Kgs. 1:33–35)

Jesus has just been hailed as the Son of David by Bartimaeus, so it is only proper that He would, like Solomon, be marked out as king by the two signs established by David. First He enters the city on a donkey; secondly, He is anointed in the environs of the city (Mk. 11:1–11; 14:3–9).[1]

We have seen in the last few chapters how Mark seems to be structuring his Gospel according to calling and restoration. The miraculous restorations are over now; there is nothing left except the ultimate restoration, the resurrection of Jesus. However, I don't think that means that Mark's Gospel has no more cycles left to its pattern. It is impossible to not notice the similarity between two stories—the sending of the two for a donkey and the sending of the two for a place to eat the Passover (Mk. 11:1–6; 14:13–15). Here we have Jesus sending two men to fulfill a task in both cases. Furthermore, not only are these passages similar to each other, but they

---

[1] I owe this and what follows to Austin Farrer, 130, 131.

are also similar to the two signs of kingship. In this case, the signs come not from Solomon's assumption of the throne, but from Samuel's prophetic signs intended to convince Saul that he was God's chosen king:

> Go into the village opposite you, and immediately as you enter it, you will find a colt tied there, on which no one yet has ever sat; untie it and bring it here. And if anyone says to you, "Why are you doing this?" you say, "The Lord has need of it"; and immediately he will send it back here. (Mk. 11:2–3)

> When you go from me today, then you will find two men close to Rachel's tomb in the territory of Benjamin at Zelzah; and they will say to you, "The donkeys which you went to look for have been found." (1 Sam. 10:2a)

> Go into the city, and a man will meet you carrying a pitcher of water; follow him; and wherever he enters, say to the owner of the house, 'The Teacher says, "Where is My guest room in which I may eat the Passover with My disciples?"' And he himself will show you a large upper room furnished and ready; and prepare for us there. (Mk. 14:13–15)

> Then you will go on further from there, and you will come as far as the oak of Tabor, and there three men going up to God at Bethel will meet you, one carrying three kids, another carrying three loaves of bread, and another carrying a jug of wine; and they will greet you and give you two loaves of bread, which you will accept from their hand. (1 Sam. 10:3–4)

Jesus thus is seen as the fulfillment both of Saul and Solomon. The first sign is easy to match because both Saul's and Solomon's signs involved donkeys. In the second case, the signs are different: Solomon is anointed and Saul receives bread intended for a sacred feast to God. But Mark recounts these two events in quick succession. First, Jesus is anointed, and then His disciples meet a man with a jug who has prepared a place for God's feast. If these two sendings of the two disciples are the beginnings of cycles, then the first cycle begins with Solomon's entry on a steed and ends with Solomon's anointing. Like Solomon, Jesus enters the city on a donkey. Unlike Solomon's rival for the throne, Jesus' rivals don't flee and surrender, but rather crucify Him.

ONLY LEAVES & NO FRUIT (11:1–26)

As Jesus enters on the back of a donkey, the people put their garments underneath Him as a kind of "red carpet treatment." In addition to their garments, they lay down "leafy branches" (v. 8).
Jesus, after hearing their heralding of Himself as the Davidic King,
looks "all around" the Temple in Jerusalem and then, refusing to
remain there, goes to Bethany for the night.

The next morning, Jesus finds more leafy branches. In this case
it is a fig tree that is not bearing figs. Jesus, as He will make clear in
the parable of the tenants (Mk. 12:1ff) is looking for more than
leaves. He wants to find fruit. The fig tree story is sandwiched
around the story of Jesus' "cleansing" of the Temple (as it is commonly called). The miracle of the withered fig tree is a parable for
Jerusalem and the people of Israel. God wants some fruit from them
and he is about to judge them because they are not producing any.

Thus, Jesus' discussion of prayer in Mark 11:22–26 is not simply a timeless exhortation to have faith and know that all prayers
asked in faith will be answered. Jesus is discussing the prayers
which the early Church will have to pray in the face of opposition
from the Temple Mount.

> Have faith in God. Truly I say to you, whoever says to *this* moun-
> tain, "Be taken up and cast into the sea," and does not doubt in his
> heart, but believes that what he says is going to happen, it shall be
> granted him. (vv 22b–23; emphasis added)

Jesus is not speaking of mountains in general. He has made a
point of saying which mountain will be cast into the sea by believing prayer. The "sea" in this case is the same sea Daniel saw in his
vision (Dan. 7; cf., Rev. 17:15). Speaking of a foreign invasion
as a drowning flood was not uncommon rhetoric for a prophet
(Is. 8:7; Jer. 47:2). Babylon is probably the ultimate example of
what happens to an evil city:

> Behold, I am against you, O destroying mountain, Who destroys
> the whole earth," declares the LORD, "And I will stretch out My
> hand against you,
> And roll you down from the crags . . .
> The sea has come up over Babylon;
> She has been engulfed with its tumultuous waves. (Jer. 51:25a, 42)

In context, it is quite clear that Jeremiah is predicting a military invasion of Babylon, not a literal flood. It is the Gentile nations who will overwhelm Jerusalem as a flood and trample the city underfoot. Just as Jesus cursed the fig tree, so will God deliver the Church through the prayers of the saints.

For this reason, it is important that the persecuted saints not become personally vindictive and hateful. Jesus warns them to forgive all personal offenses: "And whenever you stand praying, forgive, if you have anything against anyone; so that your Father also who is in heaven may forgive you your transgressions" (Mk. 11:25).

THE SIN OF ZEALOTRY

What fruit was Jesus looking for? What was he finding in its place?

When Jesus shut down Temple commerce for a brief time, He was not "cleansing" the Temple, but prophesying its destruction. Commerce was an inherent part of the central sanctuary, not due to human corruption but to divine design.

> You shall surely tithe all the produce from what you sow, which comes out of the field every year. And you shall eat in the presence of the LORD your God, at the place where He chooses to establish His name, the tithe of your grain, your new wine, your oil, and the first-born of your herd and your flock, in order that you may learn to fear the LORD your God always. And if the distance is so great for you that you are not able to bring the tithe, since the place where the LORD your God chooses to set His name is too far away from you when the LORD your God blesses you, then you shall exchange it for money, and bind the money in your hand and go to the place which the LORD your God chooses. And you may spend the money for whatever your heart desires, for oxen, or sheep, or wine, or strong drink, or whatever your heart desires; and there you shall eat in the presence of the LORD your God and rejoice, you and your household. (Deut. 14:22–26)

This law for tithing would apply to many other sorts of sacrificial occasions. When Mary sacrificed two doves or pigeons (Lk. 2:24), are we to assume that she had a private bird collection that had traveled with her to Bethlehem? It is perfectly possible that one of the dove-sellers that Jesus drove out of the Temple precincts had three decades earlier sold His mother the fowl that she offered up to God. Jesus was not cleansing the Temple, but rather forcefully declaring that it was all about to come to an end.

Jesus' statements give us further reason to believe that He was prefiguratively destroying the Temple, rather than cleansing it. When Jesus referred to the Temple as "a robber's den" He was invoking Jeremiah 7:

> The word that came to Jeremiah from the LORD, saying, "Stand in the gate of the LORD'S house and proclaim there this word, and say, 'Hear the word of the LORD, all you of Judah, who enter by these gates to worship the LORD!'" Thus says the LORD of hosts, the God of Israel, "Amend your ways and your deeds, and I will let you dwell in this place. Do not trust in deceptive words, saying, 'This is the temple of the LORD, the temple of the LORD, the temple of the LORD.' For if you truly amend your ways and your deeds, if you truly practice justice between a man and his neighbor, if you do not oppress the alien, the orphan, or the widow, and do not shed innocent blood in this place, nor walk after other gods to your own ruin, then I will let you dwell in this place, in the land that I gave to your fathers forever and ever.

> "Behold, you are trusting in deceptive words to no avail. Will you steal, murder, and commit adultery, and swear falsely, and offer sacrifices to Baal, and walk after other gods that you have not known, then come and stand before Me in this house, which is called by My name, and say, 'We are delivered!'—that you may do all these abominations? Has this house, which is called by My name, become a den of robbers in your sight? Behold, I, even I, have seen it," declares the LORD.

> "But go now to My place which was in Shiloh, where I made My name dwell at the first, and see what I did to it because of the wickedness of My people Israel. And now, because you have done all these things," declares the LORD, "and I spoke to you, rising up early and speaking, but you did not hear, and I called you but you did not answer, therefore, I will do to the house which is called by My name, in which you trust, and to the place which I gave you and your fathers, as I did to Shiloh." (Jer. 7:1–14)

The people of Jerusalem in Jeremiah's day were trusting "in deceptive words," thinking that because the Temple was in their midst that God would always protect them. God responds to this by saying that even though they have the Temple in their midst, He will destroy them and the Temple just as before He destroyed the Tabernacle at Shiloh because of the sins of Eli's sons. Indeed, Eli's sons sinned in their worship (1 Sam. 2:12–17), and so did the Hebrews of Jeremiah's day, committing abominations and then boldly drawing near to God's presence and claiming they would be delivered from the judgment they deserved when their worship only aggravated their offenses.

Jesus, then, is by one reference invoking both the judgment that fell on the Tabernacle at Shiloh and the judgment that fell on Solomon's Temple in Jerusalem. Just as the Tabernacle was replaced by a greater sanctuary, Solomon's Temple, and just as Solomon's Temple was replaced by a greater sanctuary,[2] so Jesus is claiming that now the contemporary Temple will be destroyed and replaced by yet another greater sanctuary.

But what was it about the Temple of Jesus' day that qualified it to be called a "den of robbers." In conformity to the modern phrase "highway robbery," many have assumed that Jesus was referring to the merchants. But the context gives us a more likely explanation. Jesus is about to be crucified between two "robbers" (same Greek word). In fact, the mob in Jerusalem will publicly choose as their hero Barrabas—another "robber" (Jn. 18:40) who is described as an insurrectionist and a murderer (Mk. 15:7). "Robber," then, is a rather misleading translation for those who were outlaw bandits.[3]

So the parallel between Jeremiah's day and Jesus' day is that in both ages the Temple was an inspiration for ultra-nationalism. Jeremiah's contemporaries thought that the Temple guaranteed that Judea would remain independent. Jesus' contemporaries— since they lived in occupied territory—thought that the Temple guaranteed that Judea would be liberated. The Temple was a "robber's den" in that it was made to fit into the ideology that

---

[2] Physically, the post-exilic Temple looked much less glorious than Solomon's Temple (Ezra 3:10–13; Hag. 2:3). However, God promised that he was no less present in that Temple (Hag. 2:5) and he granted Ezekiel a vision which showed the Temple would be so grand that it was beyond anything which could be architecturally reproduced (Ezek. 40–48).

[3] See N. T. Wright's *Jesus & the Victory of God* (Minneapolis: Fortress, 1996), pp 156ff.

allowed the Jerusalem mob to prefer Barrabas to Jesus and to be glad that the High Priest was publicly supporting Barrabas.

The sin of the Temple then was zealotry. But what would Jesus have rather found in the Temple? "My house shall be called a house of prayer for all the nations." Jesus is quoting from Isaiah the prophet:

> "Also the foreigners who join themselves to the LORD,
> To minister to Him, and to love the name of the LORD,
> To be His servants, every one who keeps from profaning the sabbath,
> And holds fast My covenant;
> Even those I will bring to My holy mountain,
> And make them joyful in My house of prayer.
> Their burnt offerings and their sacrifices will be acceptable on My altar;
> For My house will be called a house of prayer for all the peoples."
> The Lord GOD, who gathers the dispersed of Israel, declares, "Yet others I will gather to them, to those already gathered." (Is. 56:6–8)

Isaiah is prophesying what Israel will be like after the exile. Curiously, most Evangelicals would be prone to read this solely as a prophecy of the result of the work of Christ. Yet here we find Jesus judging Jerusalem as if it had fallen from this standard. Jesus' perspective seems to be that the foreigners were supposed to already be worshiping God on His holy mountain.

The idea that God excluded believing Gentiles from sanctuary worship in Israel is a significant error that needs to be corrected in our thinking. From the time of the establishment of the Tabernacle, believing foreigners had the same access to the altar that circumcised Hebrews had:

> Any man of the house of Israel or of the aliens in Israel who presents his offering, whether it is any of their votive or any of their freewill offerings, which they present to the LORD for a burnt offering—for you to be accepted—it must be a male without defect from the cattle, the sheep, or the goats. Whatever has a defect, you shall not offer, for it will not be accepted for you. And when a man offers a sacrifice of peace offerings to the LORD to fulfill a special vow, or for a freewill offering, of the herd or of the flock, it must be perfect to be accepted; there shall be no defect in it. Those that are blind or fractured or maimed or having a running sore or eczema or scabs, you shall not offer to the LORD, nor make of them an offering by fire on the altar to the LORD. In respect to an ox or a lamb

which has an overgrown or stunted member, you may present it for a freewill offering, but for a vow it shall not be accepted. Also anything with its testicles bruised or crushed or torn or cut, you shall not offer to the LORD, or sacrifice in your land, nor shall you accept any such from the hand of a foreigner for offering as the food of your God; for their corruption is in them, they have a defect, they shall not be accepted for you. (Lev. 22:18–25)

And if an alien sojourns with you, or one who may be among you throughout your generations, and he wishes to make an offering by fire, as a soothing aroma to the LORD, just as you do, so he shall do. As for the assembly, there shall be one statute for you and for the alien who sojourns with you, a perpetual statute throughout your generations; as you are, so shall the alien be before the LORD. There is to be one law and one ordinance for you and for the alien who sojourns with you. (Num. 15:14–16)

At the time of Jesus, the Temple had a barrier that kept out the Gentile God-fearers (cf., Acts 21:27–29). This barrier was an offense against God. Jesus is clear that the Temple was *for all the nations*. After the exile, the Hebrews became an international people who had much more opportunity to witness to Gentiles. Thus, Isaiah prophesied a time when unprecedented numbers from the nations would come to Jerusalem to worship. That time had come and gone when Jesus came to the Temple looking for that fruit.

What is true of the Temple is all the more true of the Church. We have been called out of the world to minister to the world. Yet how many unnecessary barriers do we manufacture to keep others at a distance?

JESUS' ORDINATION QUESTIONED (11:27–33)

This conflict between Jesus and the chief priests and scribes and elders is often treated simply as a tricky way Jesus evaded giving them an answer. In this view, Jesus' opponents asked Him a question He did not want to answer, so He turned the tables by asking them a question that they did not want to answer and insisted that they give an answer first.

In actual fact, Jesus gave them an answer. Jesus had been ordained and called to His ministry through John's baptism. When the priests, scribes, and elders ask about the source of His authority, Jesus could not be more direct in answering their question than by bringing up the subject of John's baptism. If they will not accept John's authority to baptize, they will not recognize Jesus' resultant ministry.

THE INVERTED PARABLE (12:1–12)

Jesus has told parables to obscure the truth; now He tells one to push it into the faces of His adversaries. Whereas before He alluded to the destruction of Jerusalem and the Temple through a reference in Jeremiah, now He tells a story that cannot be misunderstood. Those who rule in Israel are the tenants. They have been rejecting the testimony of the prophets (messengers sent by the vineyard owner) and have not given their landlord any fruit from his land.

Jesus' parable comes from Isaiah 5:1ff, but with some modifications. This time, instead of the vineyard producing only thorns, the vineyard does indeed produce fruit: fruit, however, that the powers that be in Jerusalem wish to keep to themselves. This fits in well with Jesus' previous denunciation of the Temple for not being a house of prayer for all the nations as it was supposed to be. The leaders in Israel are trying to keep the Gentiles away from God and want to keep all God's blessings for their own benefit.

What is most noteworthy, however, is the role Jesus ascribes to Himself. He is not merely a messenger (i.e., prophet), but the beloved Son and the Heir to the entire vineyard. Indeed, Jesus goes on to refer to himself as the Chief Cornerstone of an implied New Temple, which is His body. Jesus as the true Son is also the true Israel. He ultimately will take it upon Himself to produce the fruit that His father wants to taste.

PHARISEES & HERODIANS AGAIN (12:13–17)

The first and only previous time that Mark mentioned the Pharisees and Herodians together, Jesus confronted them in the synagogue and had to flee the area (Mk. 3:1ff). Now Jesus will again need to leave, this time exiting the Temple and the city and finding temporary refuge on the Mount of Olives.

Jesus has just claimed that the Temple and City are not paying their proper tribute to God. Naturally, the Pharisees and Herodians ask about paying tribute to a pagan emperor. This is a classic trap, since no matter how Jesus answers, it will get Him in trouble. Either the mob will hate Him and perhaps harm or kill Him for saying that taxes should be paid to Caesar, or else the authorities will move against Him for inciting sedition by denying that such taxes should be paid.

Jesus answers with great wisdom so as to prevent a violent reaction when He answers that yes, indeed, one should pay one's taxes to Caesar. The coin is a tangible demonstration of the blessings that flow from Rome's government. Their possession of a denarius undercuts the Pharisees' zealous insistence that one should evade taxes.

Incidentally, the principle Jesus lays down also applies to us personally as ones who ought to offer our whole selves to God. God made us and, moreover, made us bearing His likeness. We are God's and therefore ought to be rendered to God.

THE RESURRECTION (12:18–27)

Earlier, Jesus was challenged by the Pharisees regarding marriage (Mk. 10:2–12). In that case, the Pharisees chose a text from Deuteronomy to argue for no-fault divorce. Jesus went back to Genesis to provide a more accurate interpretive context for Moses' statement. Now the Sadducees challenge Jesus on the basis of the permanence of marriage, using a text from Deuteronomy to make the resurrection look silly. Jesus once again goes back earlier in the Pentateuch to answer His critics. This time He turns to Exodus to show how the resurrection is clearly established in Scripture.

NOT FAR FROM THE KINGDOM OF DAVID'S GREATER SON (12:28–37)

Soon after Jesus responded to the Pharisees regarding Deuteronomy and marriage, a rich young ruler came and asked what he must do to inherit eternal life. Now we find a scribe asking Jesus a question and Jesus responding that he is "not far from the Kingdom of God" (Mk. 12:34). In the one case, Jesus dealt with one who had earthly wealth. In this case, He deals with one who excells in the knowledge of the Word of God. In both cases the question is, "What, if anything, is lacking?" In the earlier case, the question is explicit; here it is implied.

Both Jesus and the scribe seem to agree as to what is the greatest commandment and what is it's corollary, which is found in Leviticus 19:18. So what is the scribe lacking? Why is he only "not far from the kingdom" rather than *in* the kingdom?

The similarities between the story of the rich young ruler and the scribe indicate that the thing lacking is loyalty to Jesus Himself. Jesus' question about the Christ (i.e. Anointed King) being the Son of David and yet addressed by him as Lord is a direct answer to the scribe's problem. David's Son is addressed by David as Lord because David's Son is more than merely a descendant of David. In a sense, Jesus is returning to the momentous claims He made about Himself in the parable of the tenants. He is the beloved Son who will inherit the vineyard; and all His enemies will be put under his feet.

DAVID PASSES JUDGMENT (12:38–13:2)

If David's Son is about to be enthroned and all His enemies put under His feet, then one might expect Him to pass judgment on the subjects in His kingdom. Jesus does so. Having already come to Jerusalem and found it wanting, He now explicitly reveals His verdict. The scribe questioning Him may not have been far from the kingdom, but most others are much more alienated from it. They oppress the poor while being ostentatious in their use of luxuries and their acts of cheap piety.

We need to exercise some caution here and realize that Jesus was speaking to a particular time and place. He does not say that it is always wrong to wear a nice robe or to pray for a long time. What He condemns the scribes for is doing such things on the backs of the people they are most supposed to be helping.

Having given us Jesus' judgment against the scribes, one

cannot help but wonder what particulars Jesus was talking about. The specific issue of exploiting the poor has not come up all that blatantly in Mark's Gospel. Mark seems aware of this and helps us by moving from the accusation to the evidence for the accusation. When Jesus sees the woman put her livelihood into the Temple coffer, He is not pleased. Time and again this is used as a moral story about how wonderful it is to give much to God. But for Jesus, the story is not about giving, but about exploitation. He leaves the Temple after witnessing the woman putting in her two coins, and when the disciples point out how nice the edifice looks, He assures them that it will all be torn down so that not one stone will be left upon another. As far as Jesus is concerned, a Temple built from the lives of the poor is ripe for destruction. The story of the widow's mites is the segue from the condemnation of the scribes for devouring widows' houses to the announcement that the Temple is going to be destroyed.

BE ALERT! (13:3–36)

The original Son of David built a Temple. Now the greater Son of David is prepared to tear one down.

In the first part of this chapter, I mentioned that beginning in Mark 11:2, we have two sections starting with two very similar accounts. In both, Jesus sends two men to get something from strangers whom they do not know, but who provide what is asked on the basis of Jesus' need. This seems to hint that we may have, in the rest of Mark's Gospel, two cycles, each beginning with a calling to a task. However, we now come to an incident with Jesus' three special disciples on the Mount of Olives. This reminds us of the original call of twelve disciples in which Simon, James, and John were put at the head of the list with new names (Mk. 3:12ff). Also, because Andrew is once again mentioned with them, it reminds us of the original call of the four (Mk. 1:16ff). It also puts us in mind of the Mount of Transfiguration where the three are taken up a mountain and given a special revelation. This naming of the three will occur again on the Mount of Olives (Mk. 14:26) at the Garden of Gethsemane (Mk. 14:32ff). Thus, we seem to have two double cycles:

[1] Mark 11:1ff Jesus sends two disciples to get a donkey.	[3] Mark 13:3ff Jesus warns the three to keep watch and not be caught sleeping.
[2] Mark 14:13ff Jesus sends two disciples to get a room for Passover.	[4] Mark 14:32ff Jesus warns the three they need to watch and pray, but they fall asleep.

If we remember that the last mountain in which the three were with Jesus was the Mount of Transfiguration, we see here that the themes from Mark 9:2–29 are now divided up between Jesus' prophecies on the Mount of Olives and His ordeal in the Garden of Gethsemane. First, Jesus took Peter, James, and John up the Mountain where they saw His glory revealed and were surrounded by a cloud. Then Jesus came down with them to the foot of the mountain where a demon could not be conquered because "this kind cannot come out by anything but prayer." Those two stages are distributed between these two sections. On the Mount of Olives, Jesus foretells his coming on a cloud, a cloud that the three have already witnessed. In the Garden of Gethsemane, Jesus pleads with the disciples to pray that they might overcome temptation, lest they be too weak to do so, just as they were too weak to overcome the demon.

JUDGMENT ON JERUSALEM

Jesus is asked, "Tell us, when will these things be, and what will be the sign when all these things are going to be fulfilled?" (Mk. 13:4). The context is clear: Peter, James, and John are asking about the destruction of the Temple that Jesus has just mentioned. To imagine that they would be asking about the end of the universe is completely unfounded. Jesus is spelling out for the disciples what He has been alluding to throughout His ministry: That Israel is in sin and will be judged by God who will use foreign armies to destroy them.

Everything about the Mount Olivet prophecy indicates a local fulfillment: Jesus says they will be flogged in the synagogues (v. 9), a form of persecution that was only experienced in the early history of the Church before the destruction of Jerusalem in A.D. 70.

Further, He speaks of testifying before governors and kings, which we find amply fulfilled in the book of Acts. Nothing in such statements hints that Jesus is trying to speak to people not yet born. He is giving His disciples warning about what *they* will experience. Jesus' warning is specific to those living in Judea who will be able to escape the wrath to come if they flee to the mountains (Mk. 13: 14). This could not be said of the Final Judgment. Earthquakes, famines (v. 8), and false messiahs (v. 6) are already showing up in the book of Acts (Acts 4:31; 5:36–37; 11:28; 16:25). What Jesus is discussing will happen within that generation (Mk. 13:30).[4]

> But in those days, after that tribulation, "the sun will be darkened, and the moon will not give its light, and the stars will be falling" from heaven, and the powers that are in the heavens will be shaken. And then they will see "the Son of Man coming in clouds" with great power and glory. And then He will send forth the angels, and will gather together His elect from the four winds, from the farthest end of the earth, to the farthest end of heaven. (Mk. 13:24–27)

Jesus' reference to the sun and moon comes from Isaiah 13:10, a prophecy against Babylon:

> The oracle concerning Babylon which Isaiah the son of Amoz saw.
> Lift up a standard on the bare hill,
> Raise your voice to them,
> Wave the hand that they may enter the doors of the nobles.
> I have commanded My consecrated ones,
> I have even called My mighty warriors,
> My proudly exulting ones,
> To execute My anger.
> A sound of tumult on the mountains,
> Like that of many people!
> A sound of the uproar of kingdoms,
> Of nations gathered together!

---

[4] The idea that Jesus could be referring to the Jewish race rather than that generation is contextually insupportable. In Matthew's Gospel it is even more insupportable because Matthew records woes to the scribes and Pharisees that will all fall on "this generation" (23:36). These woes are then explained to the disciples on the Mount of Olives in Matthew 24. Matthew too reports the Lord saying that all things shall come to pass upon "this generation." There is no way one can make the two meanings of "generation" differ from one another apart from exegetical violence.

The LORD of hosts is mustering the army for battle.
They are coming from a far country
From the farthest horizons,
The LORD and His instruments of indignation,
To destroy the whole land.
Wail, for the day of the LORD is near!
It will come as destruction from the Almighty.
Therefore all hands will fall limp,
And every man's heart will melt.
And they will be terrified,
Pains and anguish will take hold of them;
They will writhe like a woman in labor,
They will look at one another in astonishment,
Their faces aflame.
Behold, the day of the LORD is coming,
Cruel, with fury and burning anger,
To make the land a desolation;
And He will exterminate its sinners from it.
For the stars of heaven and their constellations
Will not flash forth their light;
The sun will be dark when it rises,
And the moon will not shed its light.
Thus I will punish the world for its evil,
And the wicked for their iniquity;
I will also put an end to the arrogance of the proud,
And abase the haughtiness of the ruthless. I will make mortal man
scarcer than pure gold,
And mankind than the gold of Ophir.
Therefore I shall make the heavens tremble,
And the earth will be shaken from its place
At the fury of the LORD of hosts
In the day of His burning anger.
And it will be that like a hunted gazelle,
Or like sheep with none to gather them,
They will each turn to his own people,
And each one flee to his own land.
Anyone who is found will be thrust through,
And anyone who is captured will fall by the sword.
Their little ones also will be dashed to pieces
Before their eyes;
Their houses will be plundered
And their wives ravished.
Behold, I am going to stir up the Medes against them,

Who will not value silver or take pleasure in gold,
And their bows will mow down the young men,
They will not even have compassion on the fruit of the womb,
Nor will their eye pity children.
And Babylon, the beauty of kingdoms, the glory of the Chaldeans' pride,
Will be as when God overthrew Sodom and Gomorrah.
It will never be inhabited or lived in from generation to generation;

Nor will the Arab pitch his tent there,
Nor will shepherds make their flocks lie down there.
But desert creatures will lie down there,
And their houses will be full of owls,
Ostriches also will live there, and shaggy goats will frolic there.
And hyenas will howl in their fortified towers
And jackals in their luxurious palaces.
Her fateful time also will soon come
And her days will not be prolonged. (Is. 13:1–22)

Babylon fell to the Medes and Persians just as Isaiah prophesied, yet the sun continued to shine and the moon is still giving its light. These poetic metaphors for the destruction of a world power were not meant to be taken literally by Isaiah, and there is no reason to think that Jesus would be using Isaiah's language differently than Isaiah. His disciples would have no problem understanding Him either, for He is quoting the Scriptures they know well.

This sort of language is by no means rare among the prophets. Here is another example, in which God is speaking through Ezekiel to prophesy His judgment on Egypt.

I will cast you on the open field.
And I will cause all the birds of the heavens to dwell on you,
And I will satisfy the beasts of the whole earth with you.
And I will lay your flesh on the mountains,
And fill the valleys with your refuse.
I will also make the land drink the discharge of your blood,
As far as the mountains,
And the ravines shall be full of you.
And when I extinguish you,
I will cover the heavens, and darken their stars;
I will cover the sun with a cloud,
And the moon shall not give its light.
All the shining lights in the heavens
I will darken over you

And will set darkness on your land,"
Declares the Lord GOD.

"I will also trouble the hearts of many peoples, when I bring your
destruction among the nations, into lands which you have not
known. And I will make many peoples appalled at you, and their
kings shall be horribly afraid of you when I brandish My sword
before them; and they shall tremble every moment, every man for
his own life, on the day of your fall."

For thus says the Lord GOD, "The sword of the king of Babylon
shall come upon you. By the swords of the mighty ones I will cause
your multitude to fall; all of them are tyrants of the nations, and
they shall devastate the pride of Egypt. (Ezek. 32:4–12)

Time and again the prophets foretell the destruction of a people
by military means using imagery of the sun, moon, and/or stars either going out or falling from the sky or changing to an unnatural
color. It is no more meant to be taken literally than a reference to
the beginning of the Nazi invasion as "the night the lights went out
in Europe" is meant to refer to a literal power failure.

What about Jesus' remark about the "Son of Man coming in the
clouds?" Here again Jesus seems to be using imagery to describe
the future judgment of Israel that was never meant to be taken literally. God said the same thing through Isaiah regarding Egypt:

The oracle concerning Egypt:
Behold, the LORD is riding on a swift cloud, and is about to come to Egypt;
The idols of Egypt will tremble at His presence,
And the heart of the Egyptians will melt within them.
So I will incite Egyptians against Egyptians;
And they will each fight against his brother, and each against his neighbor,
City against city, and kingdom against kingdom.
Then the spirit of the Egyptians will be demoralized within them;
And I will confound their strategy,
So that they will resort to idols and ghosts of the dead,
And to mediums and spiritists.
Moreover, I will deliver the Egyptians into the hand of a cruel master,
And a mighty king will rule over them, declares the Lord GOD of hosts.
(Is. 19: 1–4)

If these two passages correlate with one another, then the point
of the imagery would be that the destruction of Egypt by civil war

and the destruction of Jerusalem by Rome are not merely happen-
stance occurrences, but rather visitations of the wrath of God and
Jesus. It will be no accident that Jerusalem is destroyed, but rather
it will be a visitation of God's presence. Several times in the Scriptures, blessing or cursing by God is referred to as a "visitation" of
the Lord. When Naomi heard that the drought had ended in
Bethlehem, the narrator tells us she heard that "the LORD had visited His people in giving them food" (Ruth 1:6). And when
Hannah is given conception in answer to her prayer, we are told
"the Lord visited Hannah" (1 Sam. 2:21; cf., Lk. 1:68; also Ps. 65:9;
106:4; Jer. 27:22; 29:10; 32:5). Likewise, in prophesying destruction for the city of Tyre, God says through Isaiah that, "the LORD
will visit Tyre" (Is. 23:17). Since God appeared in a cloud with His
people, leading them through the wilderness, the imagery of God
coming in a cloud simply amplifies this concept.

However, there is another Old Testament reference that needs
to be brought into consideration. Jesus' statement that "then they
will see 'the Son of Man coming in clouds' with great power and
glory" is a direct appeal to Daniel 7:13.

> I kept looking in the night visions,
> And behold, with the clouds of heaven
> One like a Son of Man was coming,
> And He came up to the Ancient of Days
> And was presented before Him.
> And to Him was given dominion,
> Glory and a kingdom,
> That all the peoples, nations, and men of every language
> Might serve Him.
> His dominion is an everlasting dominion
> Which will not pass away;
> And His kingdom is one
> Which will not be destroyed. (Dan. 7:13–14)

What is notable here is that this passage is not about a journey on
the part of the Son of Man from Heaven to any place on earth, but
rather it is about a movement from earth up to the throne of God in
heaven. This passage refers to the Ascension of Christ, not to His Second Coming. Jesus will ascend before his disciples alone, but the
destruction of Jerusalem will be his public vindication before the

world. Daniel shows the Son of Man being enthroned and the great beast being destroyed. In Jesus' rhetoric, he is the definitive Son of Man and the corrupt powers in Israel are the beast that will be judged.

Jesus also goes on to state that the Son of Man "will send forth the angels, and will gather together His elect from the four winds, from the farthest end of the earth, to the farthest end of heaven." Again, this *cannot* be referring to a "rapture" of the saints because all of this must happen before Jesus' own generation passes away (Mk. 13:30). Rather, Jesus is using the language of the return from exile:

> If your outcasts are at the ends of the earth, from there the LORD your God will gather you, and from there He will bring you back. (Deut. 30:4)

> "They shall be carried to Babylon, and they shall be there until the day I visit them," declares the LORD. "Then I will bring them back and restore them to this place." (Jer. 27:22)

> For thus says the LORD, "When seventy years have been completed for Babylon, I will visit you and fulfill My good word to you, to bring you back to this place." (Jer. 29:10)

Notice that God promises to personally go to the exiles and re-gather them; yet the exiles were returned through the decree of a human being, Cyrus the Gentile emperor, whom God named His shepherd and His anointed (Is. 44:28, 45:1). Unlike when God led Israel out of Egypt by a cloud, God used human agency to "visit" His people and "gather" them.

Furthermore, notice that this re-gathering did not involve the geographical relocation of massive numbers of Hebrews. Most stayed where they had been settled and were (at their best) a missionary people among the Gentiles from that time on (Jn. 7:35; Acts 2:5–11). If God had literally brought them all back from the nations, then Paul's missionary journeys would never have taken place in the way they did. He went from synagogue to synagogue in Gentile lands preaching to Jews outside of Israel and to Gentile proselytes who had been converted by those Jews (cf., Acts 13:13ff). This gathering, then, involved spiritual renewal brought about in part by the rebuilding of the Temple and of Jerusalem and the re-establishment of the sacrificial system. But it did not mean that all the Hebrews were literally gathered into one place.

Building on this, Jesus prophesies that in Jerusalem's destruction, which is His vindication, the Gospel will go forth by messengers (remember that the word for "angel" and "messenger" is identical in both Greek and Hebrew). Jesus is referring to the ongoing Great Commission, not the "rapture."

Jesus concludes His prophecy with an exhortation for the disciples to "watch" (Mk. 13:37; NASB: "be alert"). These things will happen in their lifetime, within that generation, and they need to be prepared for them.

As all things in the Bible, even though this prophecy was fulfilled in the destruction of Jerusalem in A.D. 70, it still applies to us. God still judges the nations and chastises or blesses His Church through history and providence. We too, as a result of the Son of Man's exaltation to the right hand of God the Father, can be "visited" and need to be watchful and to pray that we are not caught sleeping.

PREFIGURING THE CRUCIFIXION

So far, we have considered the Mount Olivet prophecy as a prediction of the destruction of Jerusalem. However, in Mark's Gospel, Jesus' discourse seems to serve another purpose as well. When we come to the Garden of Gethsemane and the subsequent trial and execution of Jesus, we will see things that are strangely familiar.

As I've already mentioned, both here and in the garden, Peter, James, and John are especially prominent. In both accounts, Jesus exhorts them to watch. Furthermore, Jesus is called upon to testify before a ruler. He is delivered up not by a family member, but by a member of His new family, as well as denied by another. On the Mount of Olives, He warns his disciples to leave their cloaks behind and in the garden, a disciple flees naked leaving his linen covering behind (Mk. 13:16; 14:51–52). He warns of floggings and then is himself flogged (Mk. 13:9; 14:15). In both accounts, Jesus prophesies that the Son of Man will soon be seen coming in the clouds (Mk. 13:26; 14:62). The prophetic imagery of portents in the sky literally occurs over the head of the crucified One (Mk. 13:24; 14:33).

What does Mark accomplish by making sure we see these two accounts in light of each other? The Mount Olivet prophecy has two main points: 1. To exhort the disciples to be faithful in their callings despite persecution, and 2. To assure and warn them that God's judgment is going to fall on Jerusalem and the Temple. Jesus then is shown to be the true and original Apostle called by God to be faithful in the face of persecution. Jesus never calls on the disciples to do anything that He hasn't done first. More than that, He is shown to be the true Israel who willingly undergoes the curse due to His people.

This second point may be easier to understand if we divert for a moment to an incident in Luke's account of the crucifixion.

> And there were following Him a great multitude of the people, and of women who were mourning and lamenting Him. But Jesus turning to them said, "Daughters of Jerusalem, stop weeping for Me, but weep for yourselves and for your children. For behold, the days are coming when they will say, 'Blessed are the barren, and the wombs that never bore, and the breasts that never nursed.' Then they will begin 'to say to the mountains, "Fall on us," and to the hills, "Cover us."' For if they do these things in the green tree, what will happen in the dry?" (Lk. 23:27–31)

In Jesus' brief parable, a green tree is an innocent man and a dry tree is a guilty man. Jesus was accused of sedition, a crime of which he was innocent. Notice that Jesus particularly singles out the women from Jerusalem and calls their attention to their children. They will be the ones guilty of sedition, rioting and rebelling within the next forty years. If the Romans are willing to kill Jesus on the pretense that He was an insurrectionist, how much more will they be willing to crucify others who are truly rebellious. The high priest led the way in persuading the mob to prefer to spare Barabbas, the insurrectionist and killer. This religious ethic of hatred for the Gentiles will come back to haunt them. Jesus has warned them that the Temple needs to be a house of prayer for all the nations but they will bring their Temple to ruin by using it to rationalize nationalistic zeal. Yet, at the moment, it is Jesus condemned to die for the sin for which the high priest and the mob are actually guilty.

Thus, if Mark 13 is a prophecy of judgment on Jerusalem, and the primary apostasy for which Jerusalem will be judged is refusing to be a house of prayer for all the nations and a light to the world (along with other sins such as consuming widows' houses), then Jesus, by being executed for revolution against Rome, is dying for exactly the sin that characterizes Jerusalem. Jesus, as the Great High Priest, willingly takes upon himself the condemnation Israel deserves.[5] Given Jesus' plea for God to forgive those who arranged His death, it seems likely that Jesus' death and intercession gave Israel more time, thus allowing the apostles to offer the gospel again to Jerusalem (c. f. Acts).

JESUS' ANOINTING (14:1–10)

Here Mark sandwiches the arrangement of Jesus' death around the anointing of Jesus with costly perfume. Though he does not explicitly tell us that Judas was one of the leading critics of the woman who poured her perfume, nor that he was using the money for his private benefit (Jn. 12:6), he does make this incident the transition between the Pharisees looking for a way to catch Jesus and Judas providing it for them.

Both halves of this double cycle end on the theme of women giving from their substance. While Jesus does not appreciate women being exploited, He was not at all opposed to a worship of God in which the worshipper "wastes" the best that there was on God or himself. By giving over the best that she had and expending it on Jesus, the woman was offering up herself to Him. We should all be willing to do this, though the world will find it wasteful and will even become covetous. The first account ends with Jesus declaring that the Temple will be destroyed (Mk. 13:1–2). This account ends with Judas arranging to destroy Jesus.

If he can't sell the perfume for himself, then there is another way he can line his pockets.

---

[5] Note that this formulation should not be seen as opposed to the Reformed Doctrine of "limited atonement." Limited atonement refers to who will and was planned to benefit eternally from Christ's priestly work. It does not refer to temporary benefits that Christ purchased. Reformed theologians agree that the atonement benefits more than just the elect.

Calling & Coronation

T he chief priests and scribes did not want to slay Jesus during Passover, but God decreed otherwise. Jesus has been anointed, so we now come to the climax of his work and the culmination of Mark's Gospel. Jesus' enthronement is at hand.

THE LAST SUPPER (14:12–25)

As we previewed in the last chapter, Jesus once again sends out two disciples to get something for Him. Once again strangers need only be told that Jesus has need of it and they willingly give it. The first time a donkey was needed; now a room is needed for Jesus' last Passover. The triumphal entry by the King into His city necessitates a royal feast.

After sending the two for a donkey, Jesus cursed the fig tree and condemned the Temple, temporarily shutting down the sacrificial system by driving out the merchants. The Hebrew texts that Jesus quoted hinted at a new Temple, and His parable of the tenants referred to a new cornerstone in such a structure. But what exactly will replace the Temple once it is gone? Here we have our answer. Just after the sending of the two again, Jesus enacts a meal using sacrificial language. Here is the heart of the rite that will succeed and replace the old Temple system.

But first there must be judgment on the new community just as Jesus passed judgment on the old. He announces that one of them is about to hand Him over (v. 18). Then, with no move to exclude the offender, Jesus institutes what we now know as the Lord's Supper.[1]

---

[1] Luke 22:19–21 leaves no doubt that Judas participated in the meal.

A COVENANT MEMORIAL

Mark's portrayal of the rite is wonderfully simple in that he skips the portion found in Luke, which is commonly translated "do this in remembrance of me" (Lk. 22:20; 1 Cor. 11:23–25). Nevertheless, we ought to consider those words because, as they have been translated for us, they affect our intuitive understanding of the purpose of the Lord's Supper in worship. The fact is that the words could be translated just as easily: "do this as My memorial."

What difference does this make? Therein lies a story, and we need to digress a bit if we are to understand the nature of what Jesus was instituting at the last Passover.

If we say that we partake of the Lord's Supper as His memorial, we maintain not only a manward reference to the Lord's Supper, but a Godward reference as well. Yes, the Lord's Supper is a commemoration of the death of Jesus our Lord and of His and our liberation from death in the resurrection. Like Passover, and like the United States' Independence Day on the Fourth of July, the celebration reminds us of a past event that gave us our present freedom and our corporate identity.

But Passover did more than that, and so does Jesus' new rite. But before we think about Passover, let's go back even further to Genesis 9:12-17:

> God said, "This is the sign of the covenant which I am making between Me and you and every living creature that is with you, for all successive generations; I set My bow in the cloud, and it shall be for a sign of a covenant between Me and the earth. And it shall come about, when I bring a cloud over the earth, that the bow shall be seen in the cloud, and I will remember My covenant, which is between Me and you and every living creature of all flesh; and never again shall the water become a flood to destroy all flesh. When the bow is in the cloud, then I will look upon it, to remember the everlasting covenant between God and every living creature of all flesh that is on the earth." And God said to Noah, "This is the sign of the covenant which I have established between Me and all flesh that is on the earth."

Notice that the Bible does not say, "When the bow is in the cloud, then *you* will look upon it, to remember the everlasting covenant between God and every living creature of all flesh that is on the earth." No—The Lord's statement is unambiguous: "When the bow is in the cloud, then *I* will look upon it, to remember the everlasting covenant between God and every living creature of all flesh that is on the earth." According to the inspired and inerrant Word of God, the rainbow was placed in the sky to remind, not us, but Him of His everlasting covenant. It is the sign of the covenant put in place for Him to read.

Obviously, this seems impossible to us. Why would God need to be reminded? He's omniscient, after all. How could God be reminded by a created thing? He's omnipotent and the only reason a creature even continues to exist is because it He maintains it for the purpose to which He appointed it. So when God forms a rainbow in the clouds to remind Him of the covenant, that means He already knows about the covenant because that's the reason that He is forming the rainbow.

These are undeniable truths, but the Word of God tells us that, nevertheless, God forms rainbows primarily to remind himself, not us, of the covenant He has made with us. When God created the universe, He entered into a relationship with His creation—primarily through us as the representatives of the universe—that is genuine and in which He is fully engaged.

All of the objections raised against the rainbow reminding God are also applicable against praying. If God already knows what He is going to do, why should we pray? If God already knows about my suffering or the suffering of my sick child, why do I go to God and say, "My child is suffering; please lower her fever and let us both get some needed sleep"? What's the point in saying that? Is God not aware of your child's suffering? Do we think we're telling Him something He doesn't know?

And yet God has appointed you as one made in His image and whom He is making more and more like Himself to be a counselor to Him. By covenant, He is committed to interacting with us person-to-person. God really does respond to our prayers. He really is reminded by the rainbow to keep His covenant. Even though God is omniscient and omnipresent, nevertheless, such things can still be truly said of him.

Indeed, if they are not, then we're no longer talking about the God of the Bible—a God, incidentally, who was enough like us that the divine person of God the Son could assume the nature of a human being and be a human person as well as a divine one. If our basic human relationships, which entail responding and remembering at such a basic level, were all alien to God's divine attributes, then we couldn't really claim to worship a personal God. And such a being could never become one of us—a man like other men in relationship with them. But even though, for us, remembering mostly happens in the backdrop of some level of ignorance, it nevertheless is part of our bearing the image of God and corresponds to His own nature—even though He is never ignorant. Even though our responding to others presupposes that we don't already know everything that will happen, every time a parent responds to the cry of His child, He is really and truly revealing the essence of God—though God knows the future perfectly.

God answers prayer. God remembers the covenant when we remind Him of it.

Having thought about the meaning of the rainbow, we should consider Exodus 12:13-14 where God speaks of the Passover:

> And the blood shall be a sign for you on the houses where you live; and when I see the blood I will pass over you, and no plague will befall you to destroy you when I strike the land of Egypt. Now this day will be a memorial to you, and you shall celebrate it as a feast to the LORD; throughout your generations you are to celebrate it as a permanent ordinance.

For Noah, God established the rainbow as the *sign* of the Covenant and said the sign was to remind him. Here God says that the blood of the Passover lamb or goat kid was a sign for them. But for them to do what? To show to God so that He would see it and respond. And this "*memorial*," said God, is a perpetual ordinance. Before the next Passover, the Tabernacle was built so that God could dwell among His people, and the Passover victim's blood was not put on the door of their homes, but rather applied to the altar. Every year God saw that blood and was reminded to keep covenant.

Now that Christ's blood has been shed on the cross as the payment for our sins, we no longer have rites that involve the shedding of blood. That's one of the reasons (not the only one) why circumcision is no longer an appropriate way to bring somebody into the Kingdom of Priests. Baptism is now sufficient. And we no longer present blood to God from slain animals.

But don't make the mistake of thinking that before Christ came, sins were truly atoned for by the blood of animals. Violating the holiness of God cannot be compensated by animal fat or goats' blood. "You delight not in sacrifice, otherwise I would give it," writes King David. "You are not pleased with burnt offering." Like the rainbow, the blood from these sacrifices was only a memorial. God only responded to them and forgave sins because it reminded Him of His covenant promises—specifically His promise to send a Son who would indeed be able to redeem us by His precious blood.

In fact, even though blood was important to the sacrificial system, not every offering presented on the altar involved a slaughtered animal. In Leviticus 2 we find that God proscribed a grain offering. And one way that grain could be presented was in the form of a cake of flour that was baked and then brought to the altar and broken. Does that sound familiar? And then the priests partook of part of the loaf and the remainder went up to God in smoke from the altar. That portion that went up was called "the memorial portion."

When Mark records Jesus naming the wine as "the blood of the covenant," he is plugging into all these texts and many more. In the Lord's Supper, the Church reminds God of the work of Christ in His once and for all atoning sacrifice for sins. We remind God to keep covenant with us. As we do this, we cannot help but be grateful for the work of Christ, and so the term *Eucharist* ("thanksgiving"), which was coined early in church history, is quite appropriate. So is the Westminster Confession's description of the Lord's Supper as "a spiritual oblation [i.e.,offering, sacrifice] of all possible praise unto God" for His "one offering up of himself, by himself, upon the cross, once for all" (Chapter 29; Paragraph 2).

THE FAST

Before we leave for the Mount of Olives, one other statement of Jesus requires our special attention, lest common misinterpretations mislead us. When Jesus declared, "Truly I say to you, I shall never again drink of the fruit of the vine until that day when I drink it new in the kingdom of God" (Mk. 14:25), many assume He is referring to a feast that will take place after the resurrection. But this is incorrect. The Kingdom comes before the end of Mark's Gospel. It is manifested even before the resurrection. Indeed, Jesus' death takes place in the New Kingdom. As we will see in the next chapter, Jesus' fast comes to an end as He hangs on the cross: "Someone ran and filled a sponge with sour wine, put it on a reed, and gave Him a drink" (Mk. 15:32).

If Mark seems ambiguous as to whether Jesus truly and intentionally drank before giving up the ghost, then we need only turn to the Apostle John for a second witness:

> After this, Jesus, knowing that all things had already been accomplished, in order that the Scripture might be fulfilled, said, "I am thirsty." A jar full of sour wine was standing there; so they put a sponge full of the sour wine upon a branch of hyssop, and brought it up to His mouth. When Jesus therefore had received the sour wine, He said, "It is finished!" And He bowed His head, and gave up His spirit. (Jn. 20:28–30)

A couple of implications should be noted: First, this confirms the theology behind John Calvin's view that, in a real sense, Jesus' "descent into Hell" occurred on the cross before He physically died. We see this articulated in the Heidelberg Catechism:

> Question 44: Why is it added: "He descended into hell"?

> Answer 44: That in my greatest temptations I may be assured that Christ my Lord, by His inexpressible anguish, pains and terrors, which He suffered in His soul on the cross and before, has redeemed me from the anguish and torment of hell.

While it is rather embarrassing to see the plain historical meaning of the Apostles' Creed so cavalierly tossed aside, the basic perspective is correct to state that Christ suffered as our penal substitute while on the cross as a sort of living death. This doesn't mean that Jesus failed to descend into the nether realm when He died biologically (Acts 2:31), but it does explain that His suffering in our place was ended by the time that He died so that the realm of the dead ("Sheol" in the Hebrew Scriptures) could be interpreted not as further punishment but as the very hands of a loving Father whose abandonment of His Son had come to an end (Lk. 23:46).

The second implication touches on what we are doing when we gather as the Church to participate in the Lord's Supper. We are eating and drinking in the Kingdom of Heaven. Undoubtedly, this will occur in an infinitely more glorious form at the resurrection. But the same Spirit who even now communicates to us the new life of Jesus Christ and therein makes the Church a new creation, even now also causes us to eat and drink in that new creation in the sacrament of the Lord's Supper.

THE SCATTERING FORETOLD (14:26–31)

We are coming now to the singling out of the three on the Mount of Olives. We approach the end of the first half of this double cycle, but it is hard to know exactly what Mark is thinking. Before the last half of the previous double-cycle, Jesus saw the woman put all she had in the Temple coffer. He then left that place exclaiming that not one stone should be left upon another. Now He has just proclaimed that He is offering up His very body and blood to God, and verse 26 tells us that they all left the upper room singing a hymn. This could be a contrast.

On the other hand, if we are inclined to see sections as more alike than different, we notice that, next Jesus declares that the disciples will be scattered.[2] The disciples have become the foundation stones of the Church (Mt. 16:18; Eph. 2:19; Rev. 21:14). To predict their scattering parallels the future destruction of the Temple so that not one stone is left upon another. Jesus as the true Temple of God must undergo His own deconstruction. In this way, He can be reconstructed and thus re-gather the living stones (1 Pet. 2:5) around Himself as their chief cornerstone (1 Pet. 2:6). Amazingly, the New Temple will not be on Mount Zion, but in Galilee (Mk. 14:28).

---

[2] What a strange thing to declare after singing a hymn to God! How did Jesus manage to bring himself to sing when he was at the edge of such an abyss? If you ever have a problem singing a hymn at a funeral, remember your Lord singing with his disciples as he walked, step by step, toward his destruction.

Despite the ambiguity, the context indicates that this first part of the double-cycle ends with verse 31, not 26. We see this by comparing the ending of each half of the double cycle. Mark includes the reference to the hymn to show a contrast between His leaving the supper and His previous abandoning of the Temple, but the similarities are predominant.

[1] Mark 11:1–13:2 Jesus sees the woman offering all she has and declares the the stones of the Temple will be scattered.	[2] Mark 13:3–14:10 The woman anoints Jesus for burial, and Jesus speaks of Gospel being preached everywhere. Judas plots to betray Jesus.
[3] Mark 14:11–14:31 Jesus declares that the disciples will be scattered and that Peter will deny him. But He will regroup them in Galilee (from where they will presumably be sent to preach the Gospel).	[4] Mark 14:32–16:8 The women come to anoint Jesus' buried body, but an angel says that He is alive and will meet the disciples in Galilee "just as He said."

PETER'S UNBELIEF

And yet Peter refuses to believe. He publicly compares himself to his brethren and declares He is greater than all of them: "Though all may fall away, yet I will not." Unquestionably, Jesus selected Peter for a special prominent role in the initial life of the disciples. Yet that special privilege, even when bestowed through such a teacher as the Son of God himself, still led to spiritual pride. Pastors and others should take warning, both for themselves—that they may realize how their own recognition of God's real gifts to them can lead to arrogance—and for those they may select for leadership training—that they may watch out for and warn against such arrogance. Humility is everything. If you are weak, then thank God.

The depths of Peter's error are all the more revealed by his insistence that, "Even if I have to die with You, I will not deny You!" "Even if…"? Has not Jesus time and again told Peter and the others that He was going to Jerusalem to be killed? Has He not declared, "If anyone wishes to come after Me, let him deny himself, and take up his cross, and follow Me" (Mk. 8:34)? Yet Peter acts like this is merely a possibility. He is still thinking of an armed takeover where he might risk his life in fighting for His master. He does not have a clue as to how Jesus plans to enter into His reign as the messianic king.

IN THE GARDEN (14:32–52)

The contrast between Peter and Jesus could not be starker. Peter is confident that he will stand in the coming trial and sleeps. Jesus, the very Son of God Himself, is torn up with temptation and prays prostrate on the ground. Jesus' spiritual superiority to Peter did not mean that He simply faced His trials as one sufficient to whatever lay ahead. Rather, it meant that He begged God for help. If Jesus needed to pray, how much more did Peter, James, and John? How much more do we?

Suddenly, Jesus is utterly alone. His first three disciples are unable to watch and pray and are caught three times asleep at their post. One of His disciples attacks with a sword in contrast to everything Jesus has been saying about how He will bring about the Kingdom. Judas circles in for the kiss, revealing himself as the betrayer. And the "chief priests, scribes, and elders" show their true colors by leading a mob of thugs under cover of darkness. Jesus is almost certainly being ironic when He says they are coming against him "as against a robber" (v. 48). They are the ones lying in wait for innocent blood in the night. Israel's best and brightest, whether within the Jerusalem system or even within Jesus' counter-movement, are all seen at their worst and darkest. Jesus alone is the faithful Israelite.

The last verse (52) sums up the entire scene. A young man has his linen covering ripped off. This is not the first time someone tried to cover his nakedness in the garden with vegetable matter. Linen was the garment of priests. But ultimately, Israel's righteousness is as useless as fig leaves.

THE CIRCUMCISED EAR

The wound received by the high priest's slave is significant (Mk. 14:47). We have already touched on the meaning of the piercing of the ear (Mk. 7:31–37). Events here fall out by God's providence so that there is a sign to Israel—a sign that the nation needs its ears opened that the people may no longer be servants, but have the status of full sons in the household.

THE TWO TESTIMONIES (14:53–72)

Jesus is brought before the Sanhedrin and Peter follows Him and warms himself by the fire. Mark then leaves Peter at the fire, tells us about Jesus, and goes back to Peter. Jesus' testimony is sandwiched between references to Peter. The contrast between the two, which began in the garden, continues in their respective trials. Jesus is silent and refuses to answer false accusations (v. 61), while Peter pour out lies in response to true statements (vv. 70–71). Jesus is accused of blasphemy because He stated the truth (vv. 60–64), whereas Peter calls down curses on his own head in order to lie (v. 71).

THE CURSE OF CONFUSION

Some accused Jesus of claiming that He would tear down the Temple and rebuild it in three days (v. 58). John's Gospel gives us this statement from Jesus himself, made three years earlier (Jn. 2:19). But from Mark's own Gospel, most of the claim could be reconstructed. Jesus' invocation of Jeremiah 7:11 pointed to the destruction of the Temple as well as its replacement by a new sanctuary, just as the Tabernacle had been replaced by Solomon's Temple (Mk. 11:17). The parable of the tenants pointedly predicted the destruction of the Temple (Mk. 12:1–9), and Jesus' conclusion from Psalm 118:22 suggests a new Temple somehow built upon or around Himself (Mk. 12:10).

Despite these public teachings, Jesus' accusers could not get their stories to line up. In the midst of this trial, the High Priest must appeal to Jesus to speak a clear word in amidst the babble in order to reach their goal. Jesus, who has only needed to remain silent to gain victory over His adversaries, obliges the high priest. He declares Himself to be the Messiah and Son of God and so provides the needed testimony.

SACRILEGE & BLASPHEMY

Christians know that Jesus is God and that such a claim would be considered blasphemy by devout monotheists who did not accept the doctrine of the Incarnation in general or as it applied to Jesus in particular. For that reason, when we read that Jesus claimed to be the Son of God and is then accused of blasphemy, we have good grounds for thinking that Jesus has asserted His Deity and has been disbelieved.

However, Mark's testimony points to something different. Notice that it is the High Priest who asks, "Are You the Christ, the Son of the Blessed One?" (Mk. 14:61) He assumes that a claim to the title of God's anointed king, "Christ" entails a claim that one is therefore "the Son of God." But it is hard to believe that a first-century hope for a Messiah involved an understanding that He would be the Second Person of the Trinity. Rather, the title "Son of God" is a royal title for Israel's king and representative. If all Israel was God's Son (Exod. 4:22; Deut. 14:1), then so was Israel's anointed representative (2 Sam. 7:14; Ps. 89:26–27).

This is probably all that the High Priest had in mind when he asked Jesus if He was the Son of God. A little reflection on Jesus' words and deeds would have caused people to realize that Israel and Israel's king's status as "Son of God" had something to do with being created (and then renewed) in the image of God. And in view of Psalm 110:1, which Jesus Himself asked the priests to explain (Mk. 12:36), it should have become clear that God's true and final King would not be merely made in the image of God, but would rather *be* the eternal image of God (cf., Heb. 1:1–5). But nothing indicates any such reflection in the Sanhedrin.

The sad fact is that the charge of blasphemy as defined by the Sanhedrin consists of nothing more than speaking against the established order and claiming to have some authority over it. We see this in the testimony offered. The accusers claiming that Jesus said He would destroy the Temple are ineffective because the witnesses cannot agree on what actually happened. But the fact that they brought up such a charge indicates that they thought it amounted to blasphemy and was thus a capital crime.

If there is any doubt about this from Mark's Gospel, Luke puts our minds to rest. Acts 6:8–14 presents a clear case that to say "that this Nazarene, Jesus, will destroy this place and alter the customs which Moses handed down to us" amounts to "blasphemous words against Moses and God" as far as the Sanhedrin are concerned.

By merely claiming to be the Christ and to stand in judgment over the Sanhedrin, Jesus has committed blasphemy. Ultimately, for the wicked, any claim of divine authority is blasphemy against them. Mark will show us more of their mindset in just a few verses (esp. Mk. 15:32). The Sanhedrin sees a man in their own power claiming to be God's king who is saying that He will be vindicated and glorified by God against their enmity. That man, they believe, cannot possibly be God's king.

This passage ends in pointed irony. Not only does God confuse the court so they are unable to convict Jesus of their own imaginary crime without the assistance of Jesus Himself; but the accusation of blasphemy is made by one blindly committing sacrilege himself. The high priest tears His robe (Mk. 14:63), something the Law of Moses explicitly forbids (Lev. 21:10). Furthermore, tearing a robe time and again signifies the prophecy of a loss of office (1 Sam. 15:27; 1 Kgs. 11:30ff).[3]

LIBERATING A PATRIOT (15:1–15)

The Sanhedrin cannot put Jesus to death on their own authority, and rather than kill Jesus illegally they would prefer Him to be executed by Rome. Thus we have another hearing for Jesus. Pilate's question is the same as the high priest's, only without the Biblical and theological terminology: "Are you the King of the Jews?" (v. 2).

---

[3] Notice also in 1 Samuel 25:4ff, that David feels very guilty for merely cutting Saul's robe, viewing it as an assault on Saul himself, as if the robe represents the king.

What happens next reveals what sort of king the mob in Jerusalem would prefer. Pilate, not happy with giving in to the priests' jealousy, decides to present the crowd with a choice between Jesus and Barabbas, "who had committed murder in the insurrection" (Mk. 15:7). Both the priests and the people reveal what sort of leader they respect and what sort of deliverance they are looking for. The same accusers telling Pilate that Jesus must be executed for claiming to be king are siding with a murderous revolutionary against Rome. Jesus has prophesied that Rome will destroy Jerusalem and the Temple. Given this sort of open siding with violent rebels, one wonders how even those lacking prophetic insight could expect anything else to happen to Israel. Israel is in the grip of a nationalist idolatry that exalts the killing of pagans, never the serving of them.

WHAT SHOULD A KING LOOK LIKE? (15:16–39)

Mark remains on theme throughout the crucifixion of Jesus. Israel is unable to recognize her king and, by implication, her God. Even those too blind to see the possibility that God might come as a man to save Israel would affirm a connection between the character of God's king and God himself. God's king should reflect the nature and character of God.

To make this point, we see another Marcan "sandwich" that begins with Roman soldiers from Italy saying in mockery that Jesus is king (vv. 16–21) and ends with a Roman centurion saying *without* mockery that He is the Son of God (v. 39). The soldiers' initial mockery comes from the idea that no one in their power could possibly be king. Yet the centurion's statement is based on the way Jesus *died*, tortured to death on a Roman device.

In between these two ends, we have the mockery of three groups of people, all presumably Jewish, not Italian. First, we see ordinary passers-by laughing at Jesus for thinking that He could be king (vv. 29–30). Then we have the chief priests and scribes doing exactly the same thing (vv. 31–32a). Finally, the robbers themselves hurl the same abuse at Jesus (v. 32b). All of them hurl a basic challenge at Jesus that must have been a monstrous temptation: "Let this Christ, the King of Israel, now come down from the cross, so that we may see and believe!" (Mk. 15:32a)

GOD THE VICTIM

Mark shows us Israel's religious leadership unable to act any better than pagan soldiers. The soldiers torture Jesus and mock Him with a crown of thorns and a purple robe because they think it is hysterical that he, a captive, could have ever claimed to be king. And the chief priests agree. They too mockingly call Him by His true title, "Christ the King of Israel." Yet they are sure that God's king would never be humiliated by death on a cross. God would never let that happen to the true King of Israel. The passers-by are reflecting the theology they have learned from their leaders. If Jesus is King, then He will come down from the cross.

Jesus' exhortation to the disciples is now revealed to have immense and radical consequences as a critique of Israel:

> You know that those who are recognized as rulers of the Gentiles lord it over them; and their great men exercise authority over them. But it is not so among you, but whoever wishes to become great among you shall be your servant; and whoever wishes to be first among you shall be slave of all. For even the Son of Man did not come to be served, but to serve, and to give His life a ransom for many. (Mt. 10:42–45)

Jew and Gentile, priest and Roman soldier, Pharisee and Sadducee are all shown to have much in common on this dark day. They all worship power. The priests and scribes do not worship at Caesar's altar, yet they have imagined God in Caesar's image. Neither God nor God's King could ever come to serve, let alone to give His life as a ransom for many. God's King was supposed to be the destroyer and judge of Caesar, not His captive and His victim.

The third class of Jewish mocker reflects the level of the theology on display. It is a theology of outlaw rebels. The "robbers" say exactly the same thing as the people and the priests. What else would insurrectionists and murderers say? Obviously, their justification of themselves depends on their conceiving of God as one who wishes Roman throats slit. Jesus cannot possibly be God's King, or if He is, it will be revealed by His miraculous deliverance from the cross. The people and priests join with the robbers in articulating this theological ideology.

The doom to which this ideology will lead is revealed with more typical irony. Roman soldiers divide Jesus' garments up among themselves while a sign proclaims in three languages that He is king of the Jews. The king's robe represents his kingdom (cf., 1 Sam. 15:27; 1 Kgs. 11:30ff). If Jesus' garments go to Rome, so will the imperial army divvy up Israel.

THE CENTURION'S CONFESSION

Yet a Roman sees the way Jesus dies and responds by declaring Him the Son of God. Whether or not the centurion had any idea what he was saying, Mark recounts his words to show that the Gospel will be going to the Gentiles as the Kingdom is taken from Israel. We can see this by showing how Mark describes this scene in wording that brings us back to Jesus' baptism.

> And immediately coming up out of the water, He saw the heavens *torn*, and the *Spirit (breath)* like a dove descending upon Him; and a *voice (cry)* came out of the heavens: "You are My beloved *Son*, in You I am well-pleased." (Mk. 1:10-11)

> And Jesus uttered a loud *cry (voice)*, and *breathed* His last (gave up the *ghost*). And the veil of the temple was *torn* in two from top to bottom. And when the centurion, who was standing right in front of Him, saw the way He *breathed* His last (gave up the *ghost*), he said, "Truly this man was the *Son* of God!" (Mk. 15:37-39)

Mark is certain that the Father is speaking through the centurion who bears witness to the loveliness of His Son who does indeed resemble the Father perfectly, even (or especially!) dying on the cross for His people. Mark reminds us of Jesus' original calling at His baptism, and shows us that He has fulfilled His mission.

THROUGH OPPRESSION TO VICTORY

While Mark shows Jesus as God's Son even under the power of the cross while no one else can recognize him, there is one other person we see go from enslavement to blessing. "They pressed into service a passerby coming from the country, Simon of Cyrene (the father of Alexander and Rufus), to bear His cross" (Mk. 15:21).

Jesus has said that His disciples must take up their cross and follow him. Here a Roman cohort forces a man at random to do so. Oppression was very real in Jesus day. It is no wonder that people hated Rome and wanted God to drive them out. But notice that Mark knows this Simon and knows who his children are. He seems to expect his readers to be familiar with them. Paul mentions a Rufus in Romans 16:13. Apparently, Simon became a disciple—perhaps through this original encounter.

There are worse things than being oppressed by foreigners. Israel should not have lost track of her calling to be a light to the world just because of resentment against her oppressors. Christians need to keep this in mind as the "culture war" heats up. Zealotry of this sort is a stench in God's nostrils. Perhaps God has some good He is going to accomplish through those who persecute us. We need to look at the opportunity to bear our cross and follow Jesus as a blessing.

THE SIGNIFICANCE OF JESUS' DEATH

In Genesis 15 we read about God making a covenant with Abram in which animals are cut in two. "Now when the sun was going down, a deep sleep fell upon Abram; and behold, terror and great darkness fell upon him" (v. 12). God proceeds to swear an oath to Abram while passing between the halves of the animal. One of the things that seems to be going on in this passage is that God is putting a curse on Himself: He will be ripped in half like the animals if he does not fulfill his promise. (cf., Jer. 34:17–22)

When darkness comes over Jesus for three hours, we are reminded of this covenant-making event. Jesus is undergoing the curse of the covenant so that His people might escape judgment. The difference is that it is not Jesus who is ripped in half, but rather the veil of the Temple. This event provokes some theological reflection from the author of Hebrews.

Since therefore, brethren, we have confidence to enter the holy place by the blood of Jesus, by a new and living way which He inaugurated for us *through the veil, that is, His flesh,* and since we have a great priest over the house of God, let us draw near with a sincere heart in full assurance of faith, having our hearts sprinkled clean from an evil conscience and our bodies washed with pure water. (Heb. 10:19–22; emphasis added)

Rather than destroy Jesus, the covenant curse rips apart the barrier that kept God's people away from Him due to their sins. Jesus' cry, "My God, My God, why have you forsaken me?" is answered by the Church, "Who shall separate us from the love of Christ?" (Rom. 8:35).

We need to keep the particularity of these events in mind. Jesus didn't pop up just anywhere in human history or in any culture at random. He did not merely live a sinless life and then die a sacrificial death that God counted as in the stead of the people He contemplated. Rather, He came to Israel "when the fullness of time came" (Gal. 4:4). Israel was supposed to minister to and intercede for the nations (Gen. 12:1–3; Exod. 19:5–6, etc.). Israel was, in other words, supposed to deal with sin for the sake of the world. Jesus came to Israel and fulfilled Israel's calling, opening up the way into the Holy of Holies in the Temple and thus into the heavens. In one action, He both provided for the forgiveness of sins and transfigured the people of God. No longer would there be a need for a special priestly nation apart from believers of other nations. Now all must be one because the dividing barrier was broken down (Eph. 2:14).

THE WOMEN DISCIPLES & WITNESSES (15:40–16:8)

Mark now introduces a new set of disciples. While the men mostly fled, there was a sizable number of women who went to Golgotha and witnessed Jesus' death. While this is laudable, Mark seems to think they should have done more. He shifts from the women to Joseph of Arimathea who "gathered up courage" in order to bury Jesus. Mark has already established that disciples are supposed to bury their master, for we are told about it in the case of John the Baptist (Mk. 6:29). Joseph acts like a disciple, while the women wait until after He is buried and then try to bring spices to His tomb, having no idea how they will get access to the body.

Nevertheless, God grants that they become the first witnesses to the resurrection. They are given a message from an angel. His appearance is interesting. In the Garden of Gethsemane a "young man" lost his robe and fled naked (Mk. 14:51). Now we see a sign that just as Jesus has undone death, He is ready to undo the damage done to His flock. He will gather them again in Galilee just as He said.

Behaving ironically to the last, the women flee not speaking to anyone. Time and again Jesus has forbidden people to speak about Him only to be disobeyed. Now He gives His disciples a message and they are too fearful to say a word.

Epilogue

When I began this book, I was uncertain as to the relation of the ending of Mark's Gospel to the rest of the text. Many believe that Mark 16:9-20 are a later addition. The reason for this is that some manuscripts are missing these verses, and the passage seems quite different in style.

In my judgment, the textual evidence in favor of the shorter ending is not conclusive. Furthermore, who can say that Mark didn't put down his pen for a while and then add a short summary later? Or for that matter, who is to say that one of the first readers did not jot down a summary to end with and show it to Mark, who gave it his approval? There was nothing "magical" about the inspiration of much of the text of Scripture. God could have worked through such means. [1]

During the course of writing this manuscript, however, the shorter version began to look like the more likely one. After all, the last cycle before this one ends with a woman anointing Jesus' body for burial. So wouldn't the paragraph regarding the woman at the burial site who wants to anoint Jesus' body make sense as the final paragraph?

Happily, I had an opportunity of presenting some of my insights at the 2001 Biblical Horizons Conference in Niceville, Florida. There, James Jordan reminded me of what Jesus said

---

[1] Compare 1 Corinthians 1:14–16 where Paul *changes his mind* in the midst of writing his letter.

about the woman who anointed him: "wherever the gospel is preached in the whole world, that also which this woman has done shall be spoken of in memory of her" (Mk. 14:9). This indicates to me that it is quite possible that Mark felt it was appropriate to add a few lines about the Gospel going into the whole world.

RESURRECTION & COMMISSION (16:9–21)

Mark is, as he has been all along, selective in the details he chooses to relate to us. He gives us three witnesses. First, Mary Magdalene is sent. Because she is one called by Jesus to bear witness to His resurrection, Mark makes sure we know that Jesus had previously restored her so that she is now able to do this task. But the disciples do not believe her.

Next, Jesus sends two witnesses. The matter has now been confirmed by two or three witnesses (two different incidents and three people testifying about them). As a matter of law, the disciples should now believe. But they refuse.

Finally, Jesus Himself must come and bear witness to Himself in a third visitation bringing with him a stinging rebuke. [2]

But Jesus brings judgment to salvation, not to condemnation. Having confronted them with their unbelief, He recommissions them and promises them His presence, manifested by supernatural signs.

And these signs will accompany those who have believed: "in My name they will cast out demons, they will speak with new tongues; they will pick up serpents, and if they drink any deadly poison, it shall not hurt them; they will lay hands on the sick, and they will recover." (vv 17–18)

The only item on this list not found in the book of Acts is the drinking of deadly poison. It is perfectly possible that one of the disciples was forced to drink poison at some point and was miraculously spared without that deliverance being recorded in the Scriptures.

---

[2] The only other use of the word in Mark's Gospel that is tranlated "reproach" by the NASB is found in 15:32 when the two robbers were "casting the same insult at him."

There may be another significance to Jesus' promise that they will be kept safe when drinking something deadly. Mark has already recorded Jesus speaking of His crucifixion as a cup He was given to drink (Mk. 10:35–45). Furthermore, the word "poison" does not actually appear in Mark 16. The word "deadly" is not an adjective but a noun. Jesus is telling the disciples that when it comes time to drink death they shall not be hurt. This could be a promise of the resurrection after their martyrdom, but that wouldn't fit very well as a miraculous sign visible to all. On the other hand, we see in the book of Acts that the first martyr, Stephen, was given signs as he was about to be killed which interpreted his death as an ascension up to heaven. His face was like "the face of an angel" (Mk. 6:15). Just as Moses' face had glowed because he saw the glory of God, so Stephen's face shows angelic glory because he is looking up into heaven and seeing Jesus (Mk. 7:55–56). Finally, he prays that Jesus in heaven will receive his Spirit (Mk. 7:59), demonstrating that he is not going down in death, but up. Stephen drank death—the cup that Jesus had drunk before him—but ultimately it did not hurt him.

However we interpret this last of the supernatural signs Jesus lists, they are a manifestation of Jesus' presence. Mark makes this clear in this final summary:

> So then, when the Lord Jesus had spoken to them, He was received up into heaven, and sat down at the right hand of God. And they went out and preached everywhere, while the Lord worked with them, and confirmed the word by signs that followed. (Mk. 16:19–20; emphasis added)

After Elijah was taken up into heaven, Elisha's miracles elicited the response "The spirit of Elijah rests on Elisha" (2 Kgs. 2:15). So it is here. Earlier in Mark's Gospel, when the twelve disciples were sent out to work miracles, the people thought that the second Elijah, John the Baptist had been raised. "John the Baptist has risen from the dead, and that is why these miraculous powers are at work in Him"—at work, that is, in His disciples (Mk. 6:14). Jesus now fulfills all these expectations. He ascends into heaven and receives His kingdom and, as a result, commissions and empowers His servants to announce His kingdom and conquer in His name

(Dan. 7:13–14; Mt. 28:18–20; Acts 2:32–36). But unlike earthly rulers, Jesus is not reduced to waiting at His throne while His servants are off on their own. Through His Spirit, He is with them, helping them and empowering them.

In this context, we might be able to deal honestly with Jesus' statements about baptism. "Go into all the world and preach the gospel to all creation. He who has believed and has been baptized shall be saved; but he who has disbelieved shall be condemned" (Mk. 16:15–16). This text does establish that baptism is ordinarily a requirement for those who would be saved from the wrath of God. There is no way to get around this.

Let's think about what is (and is not) at stake here. First of all, this does not mean "grace and salvation are . . . so inseparably annexed" to baptism "that no person can be regenerated, or saved, without it."[3] When we read Paul telling the Romans "if you confess with your mouth Jesus as Lord, and believe in your heart that God raised Him from the dead, you shall be saved" (Rom. 10:9), we know that deaf-mutes are exempt from the requirement to verbally confess, "Jesus is Lord." There is no reason to think that Jesus has in mind the case of a convert who is somehow prevented from being baptized. Rather, He is referring simply to the ordinary ministry of the Gospel in which the Church is not only supposed to proclaim a message but to add people to the Church by the rite of baptism.

I argued in chapter 1 that John baptized in order to give people a new entrance into the Promised Land. By applying water from the Jordan, the eastern boundary of the land where Joshua had led the people into their inheritance, John was allowing people who were prepared for God's presence to be a new Israel. Paul states likewise that baptism brings us into the Church (1 Cor. 12:13). As mentioned in chapter 1, the fact that heaven has waters in it makes a transition marked by water especially significant—representing a move from earth to God's kingdom.

Through baptism then, Jesus' officially claims a new disciple. He is present and working with His Church—including at work in baptism adding people to His Church. Some who are baptized

---

[3] C.F Westminster Confession of Faith, Chapter 28, paragraph 5.

may in fact turn out to be "false sons" or apostates, just as Judas was, but they are members of God's covenant people just as Judas was one of the Twelve. Baptism is the means by which disciples are called. It is the outward-moving border of the New Israel in which Jesus' reign is recognized. It is normally the beginning of salvation.

FOR FURTHER READING

My interest in Mark's Gospel began in earnest as a result of a sermon series preached from 1996 to 1997 by Rev. Jeff Meyers of Providence Reformed Presbyterian Church. I don't know if tapes of his sermons are readily available, but he did give some lectures the following summer at the Biblical Horizons Conference hosted by James Jordan. At the time of this writing, the three audiotapes cost $40.00, and they are well worth listening to. Order them from Biblical Horizons, P.O. Box 1096, Niceville, FL, 32588.

While listening to Jeff's preaching, I discovered Austin Farrer's *Studies in Saint Mark* in my seminary library. If that book were still in print there would have been no need for me to write. His work is priceless. If you can find it, get it.

On a wider scale, I would not be able to write much about anything in the Bible without the work of James Jordan and then, later (in my own bibliographic biography), Peter Leithart. Much of Jordan's material is available free on his website (http://www.hornes.org/biblicalhorizons/). Basic hermeneutical and biblical background is given in Jordan's *Through New Eyes: Developing a Biblical View of the World*. Peter Leithart's work, *A House for My Name* is similar, but written in the format of a survey of the whole Old Testament that covers some things that Jordan's work does not. Reading both of them would help anyone studying any book of the New Testament.

Finally, I cannot recommend N. T. Wright's *Jesus & the Victory of God* highly enough. It is part two of a projected multi-volume series entitled *Christian Origins & the Question of God*. The first volume *The New Testament & the People of God* is also of great value. If you read Wright's works on Jesus you will never read the Gospels the same way again. You will never think of Jesus in the same way again.

INDEX